Battleground Europe

ORADOUR

THE DEATH OF A VILLAGE

The main

D1346977

Battleground Europe

ORADOUR

The Death of a Village

Philip Beck

Pen & Sword
MILITARY

First published in Great Britain in 2004 by
Pen & Sword Military
an imprint of
Pen & Sword Books Ltd
47 Church Street
Barnsley
South Yorkshire
S70 2AS

ISBN 1 84415 100 X

A CIP catalogue record for this book is
available from the British Library

Typeset in Palatino 10pt

Printed and bound in the United Kingdom by CPI

Pen & Sword Books Ltd incorporates the Imprints of Pen & Sword Aviation, Pen & Sword
Maritime, Pen & Sword Military, Wharncliffe Local History, Pen and Sword Select, Pen and
Sword Military Classics and Leo Cooper.
For a complete list of Pen & Sword titles, please contact
Pen & Sword Books Limited
47 Church Street, Barnsley, South Yorkshire, S70 2AS, England
E-mail: enquiries@pen-and-sword.co.uk
Website: www.pen-and-sword.co.uk

CONTENTS

Acknowledgements
I am specially grateful to Michael Williams for allowing me to use material from his website on Oradour. Also to the Bundesarchiv, the Taylor Library, John Moore and Philip Vickers for pictures. My daughter Stephanie has been especially helpful with secretarial services.

Bibliography
Petite Histoire d'Oradour-sur-Glane, Albert Hivernaud; *Oradour-sur-Glane, Vision d' Epouvante,* Guy Pachou and Dr Pierre Masfrand; *Trafics et Crimes Sous l'Occupation,* Jacques de la Larue; *Dans l'Enfer d' Oradour,* Pierre Poitevin; *Crimes Ennemis en France,Oradour-sur-Glane* (Archives du Service de Recherche des Crimes de Guerre Ennemis); *Le Scandale d'Oradour,* Raymond Carter; *Madness at Oradour,* Jens Kruuse; *Das Reich,* Philip Vickers; *Das Reich,* Max Hastings.

PREFACE

On 10 June, 1944, four days after the landing of the Allied armies in Normandy, while the attention of the world was focussed on the progress of the greatest battle in history, an appalling crime was committed by the SS, hundreds of kilometres away in central France. Though not unique in the history of that army of ruthless killers, it shocked the world when, after the liberation of France, the full extent of what had happened was revealed. A detachment of the 2nd SS Panzer Division, known as *Das Reich*, on their way from the south to the battlefield, sacked the village of Oradour-sur-Glane, near Limoges. They killed 642 men, women and children and destroyed every building by fire.

The members of the detachment, composed of Germans and Alsatians, mostly between the ages of 17 and 25, descended on the village on a sunny Saturday afternoon. The people were discussing the news of the Normandy invasion with the hope of early liberation from the German occupation. A number of refugees and weekend visitors had swelled the population. The village had no record of maquis activity and there had been no action in the immediate vicinity for which a reprisal might have been feared. In fact, the people were quite unconscious of what was about to happen.

This is a revised and enlarged version of my book *Oradour – Village of the Dead*, published in 1979. It is the result of further research and careful consideration of all the reports and opinions on the massacre. New material includes the trial of the only officer, among those involved in the raid, to be captured. This was in 1983. He had returned to his home in East Germany after the war, without changing his name, and despite an extensive search for war criminals, had been overlooked until nearly forty years later.

Another important addition concerns the actions of the *Das Reich* Division during their march. They had received orders to travel to the Normandy battlefield, crushing all resistance en route. They were frequently ambushed and attacked by maquisards, under orders from London, and lost both men and material, so that they were bloodied and revengeful when they arrived at Limoges. This has to be borne in mind when

Battle hardened men of *Der Führer* Regiment, 2 SS Panzer Division *Das Reich* in action on the eastern front. In June 1944 they were unleashed against French civilians at Oradour-sur-Glane.

considering the reasons for the massacre.

Other new material includes the mysterious fate of General Gleiniger, the German officer in charge of the Limoges district, and the arrest and imprisonment of the Bishop of Limoges. There are also additional reports by survivors and details of the salvage work and the vain efforts to interest the Vichy government.

The feelings of the young soldiers as they killed and burned the people – particular1y the women and children in the church – are almost impossible to realise. So many of them vanished after the war and the few who were tried at Bordeaux in 1953 gave contradictory accounts and seemed unmoved by what they had done. When they had finished with Oradour, the soldiers moved off to their billets in another village, drinking looted liquor and singing. Did the SS always manage to wipe out of their minds the atrocities they committed? Rudolf Höss, commandant of the Auschwitz concentration camp, wrote in his memoirs,

> *'When the spectacle was too shocking I could not return home immediately to my family. I either mounted a horse and galloped the horrid images out of my mind or, at night, I went to the stables and found peace among my dear horses.'*

After which he returned to his pleasant house outside the wire. The effect of the Oradour slaughter on the minds of the survivors and the bereaved – particularly the parents who lost all their children – can only be imagined.

Many of the bereaved received psychiatric treatment. But what can have been their attitude to religion, when the hundreds of women, locked in the church with the children, prayed fervently for their menfolk without realising that they themselves were to be slaughtered in an appalling fashion in the sanctuary of the house of God? Did such an utter failure of mass prayer have no effect on the religious belief of the bereaved?

In the film *Le Vieux Fusil* which deals with a similar SS massacre a man who lost his family is seen entering the church and, on finding it littered with bodies, smashes the figurines and other emblems of the Christian Faith. I wonder if the bereaved of Oradour were tempted to do the same to the emblems in their church which had not already been shattered by the soldiers.

One of the men who survived the fusillade in a barn said, when interviewed fifty years later, that the 'Boches' were the guilty ones and he bore no ill feelings against the present generation in Germany. However, as an afterthought, he added that he would not like to meet a German in Oradour.

One of the mysteries that remain unsolved is why a party of soldiers went to the ruins on 12 June, with orders to make a token burial of the dead. They dug trenches in several places and threw in as many bodies as they would hold. One of the accused at the Bordeaux trial, an Alsatian, said he was one of the burial party but could give no reason for this strange action.

Someone in the division may have had a strong enough feeling of guilt to create a rearguard for the purpose, while the rest of the division continued their journey northwards. On the other hand, the 'token burial' may have been carried out by members of the 19th Regiment of SS Police stationed in Limoges, acting on the orders of a *Das Reich* officer.

Captain Kahn, one of the leaders of the raid, is said to have ordered the killing of a woman who tried to save herself by appealing to him in German, because he 'wanted no witnesses' of what he and his men were doing. But surely he must have realised that the full extent of the atrocity would inevitably be known, whatever form of cover-up he might employ? The Limoges Gestapo sought the survivors, apparently to stifle their testimony. Fortunately, with the help of the Resistance, none of these shocked, frightened people were traced.

One thing worth pointing out is that the SS were not always responsible for the atrocities attributed to them. The German Army (*Wehrmacht*) and some of the maquisards could be equally ruthless.

An exhibition of some of the atrocities committed by the Army in the Second World War was staged in several cities in Germany and Austria fifty years after the end of the war. It provoked protests by army veterans, and Neo-Nazis, particularly in Munich, the birthplace of the regime.

I have used the British Army equivalent of the SS ranks which, I believe, makes easier reading (e.g. *sturmbannführer* – major).

The forces of the Resistance had many different titles. They were variously known as Maquis, Partisans, Franc-Tireurs, AS, FTP, FFI, MUR, etc, and I have only used their titles when it was clear who was involved in a certain action. Otherwise I have simply called them maquis, maquisards or members of the Resistance.

I have used the word *mairie* instead of town hall as most of the villages had a *mairie* and it would be inappropriate to call it a village hall.

PHILIP BECK, *Saint Malo, February 2004.*

PROLOGUE

Nothing in the life of Oradour-sur-Glane, a village about ten miles north-west of Limoges, was anything like as spectacular and dramatic as its death. It survived the religious wars and revolutions. The biggest blow was the 1914-18 war in which nearly a hundred of its men died, but the village itself was unscathed.

The name Oradour means 'place of prayer'. In the Limoges region there are other Oradours, such as Oradour-sur-Vayres and Oradour-Saint-Genest. The origin of the church of Oradour-sur-Glane is unknown although the oldest part is manifestly 12th century. The nave and side chapels date from the 15th century. The tower, which supported the now-vanished steeple, was fortified during the religious wars, in common with other churches, when they became strongpoints.

The cemetery contains a *lanterne des morts* of the 12th century. It is one of only seventy-five in France. Seven of these are in Haute-Vienne, the Department in which Oradour is situated. The Oradour lanterne was moved to its present position in 1773 when the old cemetery on the left bank of the River Glane was closed by Charles de Lescours, the lord of the manor. He did not like having a burial place near his manor and offered the village another piece of land on its boundary. He was supported by other landed gentry in the district and the Bishop of Limoges approved the consecration of the new site. However the villagers were strongly opposed to the change and horrified by the prospect of moving the remains of their ancestors, together with their headstones. The people still tried to bury their dead in the old cemetery so the marquis ordered the planting of a hedge of trees and the digging of a deep ditch to discourage further attempts. The people uprooted the trees and filled in the ditch. The cemetery war, which started in 1772, went on until 1783 when the people had to admit defeat. Towards the end, the matter

The 12th century *lanterne des morts* in Oradour-sur-Glane cemetery.

10

was debated in Parliament and it was decreed that the costs involved in the litigation should be paid by the villagers in proportion to each householder's tax rating.

The ruins of Oradour have two places named *Champ de Foire*, which means fairground or market place. The largest is in the centre, just off the main street, and was used by the SS for the round-up of the population prior to their massacre. The other, a shaded lawn, is on the right side of the entrance. The first fairs date from 1563. At the request of the lord of the manor it was decreed, by letters patent of King Charles IX, that there should be four fairs a year in Oradour and a market every Monday.

At first the lords of the manor benefited considerably by taxes imposed on the traders. The Revolution of 1789 put a stop to this practice. Otherwise, the Revolution hardly affected Oradour, although the local aristocracy suffered. Six weather vanes (a weather vane was a privilege of nobility) were removed from the Lescours Château but it escaped the burning suffered by other big houses.

The population has declined during the past century, probably due to the shift to the cities in search of work and better wages. It had reached 1,952 in 1662 and was 1,591 in 1830. In 1944, although inflated by refugees, it was under 1,000. The first school was established in 1330 when the mayor was Jean Desourteaux, whose family name became associated with several mayors.

A tramway, linking the village with Limoges, Saint-Junien and Bussière-Pointevine, was laid in 1911 and brought electric

This picture of the tram station at Oradour, taken about 1930, includes the conductor and female stationmaster. The tram (more like an electric train) has a trailer for transporting goods. Another trailer could be used for passengers.

light. Street lamps were installed in 1937. Five trams passed daily in each direction. It took one and a quarter hours to get to Limoges, many stops being made en route.

In 1939, Oradour was chosen to accommodate 400 people evacuated from Schiltigheim, a small town near Strasbourg, but after the armistice with the Germans in June 1940 most of them returned home. They were replaced by sixty people expelled from Lorraine. They were mostly from Charly and Monton-Flauville, near Metz. After the war, Charly became Charly-Oradour to commemorate the local victims of the massacre.

In 1944 some people regarded Oradour as a town. It had a mayor and *mairie*, a post office, a tram station, a bank, a dozen inns, three cafés and four hotels. But the area it covered was comparatively small.

It had a surprising number of trades. There were two bakeries, two butchers' shops, three charcuteries (pork butchers), four hairdressers, five haberdashers, two hat shops, two cobblers, two tobacconists, two garages, four wheelwrights, two ironmongers, three shoe shops, six timber merchants and a pharmacy.

Although most of the people were of modest means, making their livelihood on the land, there was a number of professional people who had their offices in Limoges. There were some fine houses and villas with large gardens. There were two music groups and two societies for old soldiers – *Les Mutilés du Limousin* and *Les Combattants du Limousin*.

It was a generally happy place with little crime. A tobacconist's had been raided during the war but there had been no attacks on collaborators, although it is believed that there were a few in the village. Military traffic had kept to the main roads. German officers had occasionally visited the village to dine at the hotels and restaurants where black market food augmented the local produce.

Ninety-seven men of the village gave their lives in the 1914-18 war. In the short campaign of 1939-40 four were killed and thirty-two made prisoners. Fourteen were deported to Germany for forced labour. They thought they were unlucky but returned to find that they had been spared an inconceivable disaster. Their homes no longer existed and their families and friends were dead.

CHAPTER 1

The Ruins

The name Oradour-sur-Glane means nothing to most people living outside France, even if it is linked with an appalling massacre. I have even met French people who admit ignorance of it. Most concise histories of the Second World War include Lidice and the reason for its extermination. But Oradour is strangely overlooked, perhaps because the motive is still controversial.

I first read about the massacre in a French magazine and was amazed that I had not heard of it before. I was shocked by the details of the slaughter of so many people and, when I read that the ruins had been preserved, being an investigative journalist, I felt that I had to go there, to try to find out what really happened.

It was the start of a long period of research. According to the map, I had to head for Poitiers and take the Route Nationale 147 to Limoges. Travelling towards Limoges, I saw many signposts bearing names which meant nothing to me. I was beginning to think I had missed the turn and would soon arrive in Limoges.

Entrance to the village shortly after the installation of the tramway (note the size of the tree behind the four figures).

A view of the church at the main entrance to the ruins.

Then, suddenly, there it was, ORADOUR-SUR-GLANE, with nothing to indicate that it was vastly, terribly different from the other villages.

Reality presented two immediate surprises: the warm colour of the ruins, intensified by the evening sun, and the proximity of the church to the main entrance. I had visualised it at the far end. The new village, off to the left, was a cluster of modern, buildings dominated by a large church with a tall, square-cut tower. To anyone who doesn't know the full terrible story the ruins may seem little more than a curiosity. They are enclosed in a low wall and have three gated entrances that are locked at night.

At each entrance there is a sign which reads simply: SOUVIENS-TOI. REMEMBER. Another sign says visitors should be correctly attired, conduct themselves with decorum, and not go into the houses. Dogs are excluded.

Entrance is free.

The first group of buildings, on the right flanking a pleasant green with trees, bears the notice <u>SILENCE</u>. The roofless church, which once had a steeple, dominates the main entrance. It was

14

the scene of the worst act of the tragedy: the slaughter of hundreds of women and children whose screams were heard for miles around. One can see the window, identified by a tablet, through which Madame Rouffanche, the sole survivor, escaped. The grille which once covered it is still bent outwards, marking the passage of her body. There is a large tablet near the main entrance which tells what happened in the church. It has been fixed to the wall near a crucifix which, claims the inscription, was unscathed.

The remains of a sewing machine.

The main street, the Rue Emile Desourteaux, is still bordered on the right, as one ascends between the ruined houses, by the tramlines which linked Oradour with Limoges. The roofless tram station where the line branches into two tracks is about midway up the street.

As one walks through the ruins a feeling of desolation is augmented by one of a sudden extinction of life, as at Pompeii. The whole population, apart from a few who miraculously got away

Plaque outside the bakery of Thomas Ragon. Note the misspelling.

after the arrival of the SS, died during the afternoon. They were taken from their homes in that picturesque place – even in ruins it is far more attractive than the new village – just after lunch on 10 June, 1944 and herded like cattle to their deaths.

In the ruined kitchens are the remains of saucepans, frying pans, coffee grinders and other utensils, abandoned just as lunch had finished, or even while the meal was being prepared for those who worked late on the land. Garages contain the rusty wrecks of cars. Fire-buckled bicycles hang from nails an walls. No one had a chance to use them to escape. Some houses contain rusty sewing machines, a few of which seem to have been purposely placed on window sills to display the industry of their dead owners. It was a busy little rural community. Unfortunately in these days of widespread vandalism, souvenir hunting and the cynicism of some young people towards the ruins it is likely that over the years some of these things have disappeared. It should not be difficult to gain access after dark.

The *Champ de Foire*, the village green where the people were assembled by the SS, is on the right of the main street going up. It must have been a delightful place before the war with its varied architecture, trees and covered communal well. Now it is bordered by the empty shells of houses, one of which bears a plaque telling of the assembly.

On the grass are the rusty, wheeless remains of the car which belonged to the village doctor who arrived back from his rounds just as the round-up had been completed. He joined the others. Across the green lie the memorial grounds. A wide, hedged lawn leads to a bench-like arrangement of stones on the roof of a crypt. The crypt contains stone tablets bearing the names and ages of all the victims. In side chambers are display cabinets set in stone holding personal possessions found among the charred human remains: wedding rings and other jewellery, watches,

A notice inside the main entrance. Silence is difficult to observe in a party.

The Hotel Beaubreuil (nearest ruin) in the main street.

pocket knives, a cigarette case pierced by a bullet, a denture and other such items. Most have been distorted by fire.

Beyond lies the cemetery, dominated by a column which marks the communal grave of 642 people. The stone platform bears two glass-topped coffins in which is displayed a collection of blue-grey human bone fragments. The most pitiful sight is, of course, the family tombs bearing inset photographs of the dead. Whole families are pictured with inscriptions after their names indicating that they were 'killed' 'massacred' or 'burned' by the 'Nazis' or 'Germans' on 10 June 1944. Some of them bear plastic or porcelain flowers. Some are garish and blatant in their silent expression of grief. The more discreet – such as a plain stone with a single picture of a pretty girl embedded in it and an inscription giving only her name and dates of birth and death – are the most impressive.

People walk quietly about the cemetery peering at the inscriptions. Children read them aloud without understanding their full implications. Some pose against headstones to be photographed.

Six tablets in various parts of the village identify the

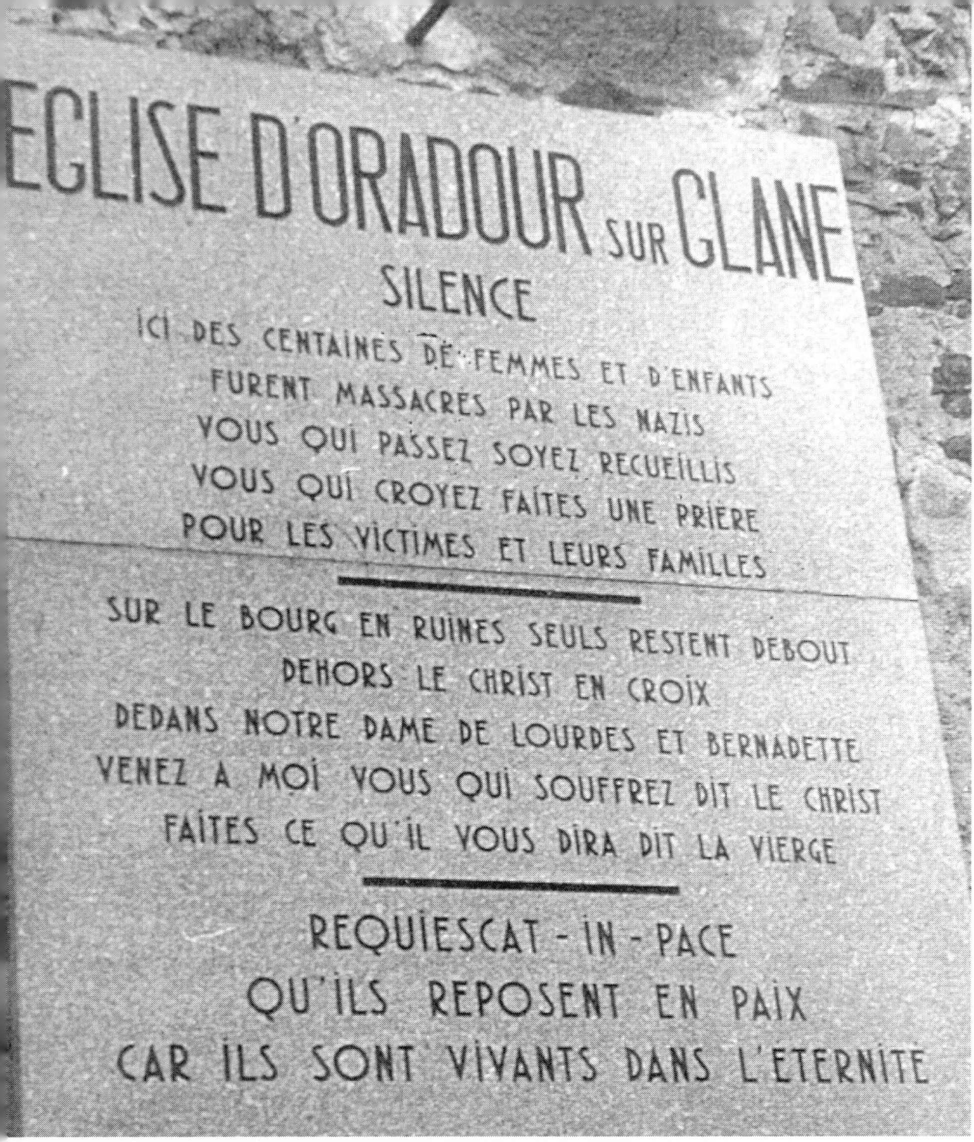

ÉGLISE D'ORADOUR SUR GLANE

SILENCE

ICI DES CENTAINES DE FEMMES ET D'ENFANTS
FURENT MASSACRES PAR LES NAZIS
VOUS QUI PASSEZ SOYEZ RECUEILLIS
VOUS QUI CROYEZ FAITES UNE PRIERE
POUR LES VICTIMES ET LEURS FAMILLES

SUR LE BOURG EN RUINES SEULS RESTENT DEBOUT
DEHORS LE CHRIST EN CROIX
DEDANS NOTRE DAME DE LOURDES ET BERNADETTE
VENEZ A MOI VOUS QUI SOUFFREZ DIT LE CHRIST
FAITES CE QU'IL VOUS DIRA DIT LA VIERGE

REQUIESCAT - IN - PACE
QU'ILS REPOSENT EN PAIX
CAR ILS SONT VIVANTS DANS L'ETERNITE

Notice outside the church reads:

Here hundreds of women and children were massacred by the Nazis. You who pass by, think of them. You who are believers, pray for the victims and their families. All that remains standing outside is the Cross of Christ. Inside is the statue of Notre Dame de Lourdes and Bernadette, 'Come to me, you who are suffering.' said Christ. Heed these words says the Virgin.

buildings in which all the men were lined up to be shot. Each bears the inscription:

ICI LIEU DE SUPPLICE. UN GROUPE D'HOMMES FUT MASSACRE ET BRULE PAR LES NAZIS. RECEUILLEZ-VOUS (Place of execution. A group of men were massacred and burnt by the Nazis. Think of them.)

They are barns, garages and a smithy. In some, bullet holes can be seen in the brickwork. A large barn or coachhouse in the Rue du Cimetière is identified as the place from which six men escaped – the only survivors of the fusillades which killed 190 men. Five of them got out through a hole in a door at the rear. A sixth tried another way out and was later found dead, halfway through a fence.

There is a tablet outside a gutted bakery, (one can still distinguish the sign BOULANGERIE over the shop window) telling that human remains were found in the rusty ovens one can see inside. A farmyard well is identified as the tomb of a number of unknown people.

In the gardens at the rear of the houses are wells, many still holding water. There was no piped water in the village so there are privies, mostly two-seaters, at the bottom of the gardens.

An untended vine climbs a dead wall to a bathroom which still has its iron bath. A rusty gate into a lane has been pierced by bullets. Several people were found hiding in their gardens and shot on the spot. Some of the houses bear tablets commemorating their inhabitants. One, fixed to the ruins of the home of the mayor, Dr Jean Desourteaux, and his son, Dr Jacques Desourteaux, has been contributed by the *Association Amicale des Médecins du Maquis et de la Resistance.*

The most awe-inspiring sight is, of course, the interior of the church. It is calm and open to the sky. Yet anyone with any degree of sensitivity must surely feel the atmosphere and visualise the terrible event that occurred there. There is a battered pram in front of the damaged altar, a symbol of the many in which babies soon to be slaughtered were wheeled into the church by their frightened mothers. On the right, as one faces the altar, is the door against which a pile of burnt bodies was found. On the left, next to the altar, is the door to the vestry which was burst open by frantic, screaming women and children trying to get away from the asphyxiating fumes of the smoke-generating device that the SS placed in the nave. The

The bakery where two bodies were found in the oven.

door has been replaced and is locked.

The window through which Madame Rouffanche made her escape is directly behind the altar. In the left transept is a chapel with a small altar which is less damaged. Behind it is a wooden confessional which miraculously escaped damage by the flames. Yet the heat was so intense that it melted the bells which are now nothing more than a mass of distorted bronze near the main entrance. A uniformed guide tells the terrible story as a sort of recitation to the curious visitors. The church is kept locked when he is not around.

The ruins comprise a total of 254 buildings. They have been preserved as a unique and immensely impressive monument to the dead. But not everyone agrees with this. Young people, particularly those with German friends, tend to regard the ruins with disdain. In fact, many people think the village should have been rebuilt. The Germans offered to do this after the war. Others feel that the village should have been restored, with the exception of the church which should be kept as a permanent memorial. It would certainly have been a more picturesque village than the new one. The new village was completed in 1953 but it took years to achieve full occupation, which is understandable. The establishment of two factories helped to attract residents. However, there were many disputes over inheritance rights. In so many cases direct heirs had died and distant cousins turned up to claim their inheritance.

Madame Rouffanche spent most of her long life in a cottage in the new village. Although her right arm and leg had been crippled by bullets she made an annual visit to the church where the rest of her family (except her husband) died. She spent the last years of her life in an old people's home and died in 1988 at the age of 91. Almost the entire population of the new village turned out for her funeral in a heavy storm. She was buried in the cemetery of the old village where her family lie.

The *Champ de Foire* where the people were assembled before being escorted to the execution sites.

The remains of Doctor Desourteaux's car on the *Champ de Foire*.

Ruins bordering the *Champ de Foire*.

The shell of a villa on the *Champ de Foire*. Possibly the home of a commuting businessman.

An execution site. The plaque reads:
A place of sacrifice. A group of men were massacred and burnt here by the Nazis.

Doorway to a hall showing tiled floor.

The car of of Doctor Desourteaux in front of the Milord ironmongery. Note the gas-generating apparatus at the back. It provided combustion instead of petrol, (compare with the picture of the car on the *Champ de Foire* where it seems to have been stripped of its gas apparatus and moved to another position). This is one of the photographs taken by Pierre Poitevin, the Limoges journalist, while there were still soldiers in the ruins.

The wreck of a car at the junction of the main street with the road leading to Saint-Julien.

Today the new village is a prosperous community with hotels, restaurants, a supermarket and a tourist office. The main attraction is the *Centre de la Mémoire* (Memorial Centre) situated just outside the village. Opened by President Jacques Chirac in April, 1999, it contains photographs, documents, maps and memorabilia, concerned with the massacre and other events up to the Bordeaux tribunal in 1953. There is also a history of the Nazi regime and the progress of the war before and after Oradour.

During the night of 27 December 1999 a hurricane swept over France, causing great damage in all parts of the country. The ruins were hit in several places and, for the first time in nearly sixty years, were closed to the public. Extensive work was required to make the buildings safe. But the closure only lasted a week.

The monument to the 642 dead. Memorial plaques can be seen in the background.

One event unconnected with the massacre is worthy of note. On the night of 23 November, 1943 a crippled Wellington bomber of the RAF made a forced landing near Oradour. The six members of the crew were sheltered in the village for three nights before the Resistance arranged their transport to Toulouse before crossing into Spain. They all returned safely to Britain.

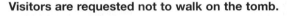

Visitors are requested not to walk on the tomb.

ICI REPOSE
la FAMILLE DESBORDES-RIBETTE

JEAN
DESBORDES
1898-1944

Marg...DESBORDES
née RIBETTE
1901-1944

LUCIEN
DESBORDES
1927-1944

LOUIS
DESBORDES
1930-1944

JEANNE LACROIX AGÉE DE 71 ANS
BRULÉE PAR LES S.S. LE 10 JUIN 1944

SE mon ÉPOUSE
MARCELLE
RATIER
29.9.1917

SE ma PETITE
ANNIE
7.9.1938

MARTYRES
du 10 Juin
1944

A ma Fille
Marguerite SIMON
Victime du massacre
30 Sept. 1932 - 10 Juin 1944
Priez pour Elle

À la MÉMOIRE de nos Chères FILLETTES et ...EURS
Ravies à Notre Affecti...

✝

CLAUDINE
13 ans

RENÉE
10 ans

HUGUETTE
7 ans

MARYSE
6 ans

Elèves de l'Ecole d'ORADOUR-sur-GLANE
Massacrées et brûlées dans l'Eglise,
Par les hordes nazies, le 10 Juin 1944.

CHAPTER 2

The Massacre

On Saturday 10 June, 1944, Oradour-sur-Glane was unusually full. In the preceding years, refugees from Alsace-Lorraine and Franco's Spain had sought sanctuary there. The visitors included people from Limoges who came in search of food, such as eggs, which was more easily obtainable in the country. A number of anglers had arrived with hopes of good sport in the River Glane. People from the neighbouring hamlets and farms had come to do their shopping and collect their tobacco ration which was distributed every ten days.

The most tragic aspect of the population was that the schoolchildren, nearly 200 in all, had not gone home that afternoon because there was to be a medical inspection and vaccination.

A light-hearted mood prevailed. The people chatted about the

Entrance to the village in 1938. Note the size of the tree behind the car. Compare its growth with the earlier view in the same position.

Rue Emile Desourteaux in 1932. The entrance to the *Champ de Foire* is just beyond the first pole on the right.

landings in Normandy, the news having been received on their radios from the BBC. The weather was fine, the food and wine in the hotels and restaurants were good and the diners speculated how long it might be before France was liberated. A few people spoke of troop movements in the locality but it was assumed they were on their way to the Normandy battlefront and would no longer harass the population of that area. They had been seen in Saint-Junien, about six miles away, but no convoys were expected to pass on the narrow roads around the village.

It was the eve of a religious festival with a First Communion service.'The church was decorated with flowers and the little communicants had had their special costumes prepared by their mothers. In the homes the mid-day meal was late because the men had been working in the fields and had not long returned from a full morning's work. At the Hôtel Milord, which still had a varied menu in spite of the shortages, the diners included a party of twenty. Some had arrived the previous day and were staying the weekend. There was a young pelota champion from Marseilles and a woman who had returned to Oradour to pick up some silver and other valuables from her home there. The guests at the Hôtel Avril included a woman with her three children and her little niece. She had come to Oradour from Paris where she feared there might be a bombardment.

The anti-Franco Spaniards who had feared reprisals when the dictator took over the government had found employment as farm labourers, mechanics and hotel staff.

A family named Lévignac who lived in Avignon, perturbed by the bombing, in that town had evacuated their sons Serge (16) and Charles (12) to Oradour where they felt sure they would be safe. The elder boy was billeted with a farmer just outside the village while the younger lived with an 80 year old woman and her daughter who was nearly 60.

M Lévignac, an insurance agent, arrived in Oradour on the 9th and stayed overnight at the Hôtel Avril. He spent some time with his sons on the morning of the 10th then took the tram to

The Rue des Bordes with the Café de la Chêne in the background.

29

Taking it easy in the sunshine. A group outside a little café in the main street.

Limoges on business. He said he would be back in the early evening. He sent a postcard to his wife in which he wrote, 'I feel I am giving our sons life itself.'

Also in the village that day were the two sons of Professor Forest, a teacher of philosophy who was a native of Oradour. He had moved with his family into a wing of the Château de Laplaud, rented to him by the Vicomtesse de Saint-Venant, a family friend.

With him were five of his six children. The professor had sought peace and quiet in Oradour when his university, in common with others, had been closed by the Germans in March 1944. The château was about two miles from the village and Michel Forest (20), who was studying law, and his brother Dominique (6), the family favourite, walked to Oradour early in the afternoon.

Michel was a poet and deeply religious. He kept a diary in which he wrote: 'This place (Oradour) is pervaded by a classic tranquillity in which one can live as a human being should.' Another entry read: 'I shall die young. But does it matter?'

The two often went for walks together. Dominique, a gentle affectionate lad, was going to take his First Communion in Oradour church on 11 June. He had to look his best, so he was going to have his hair cut by a village barber and would also visit his grandfather.

Professor Forest went to Limoges by tram, accompanied by his other sons, Jacques, Bernard and François.

A brother and sister from Strasbourg, Emile and Odile Neumeyer, were staying with the parish priest, the Abbé Chapelle, aged 70. He was poor and humble and had to take care of himself when his aged housekeeper died.

The Abbé Chapelle had been obliged, since the war, to extend his ministry to Javerdat, about three miles west. Despite his age, he walked there every morning whatever the weather, to say Mass.

The Neumeyer family were for a time refugees living in a house near the presbytery. When most of them decided to return to Strasbourg, Odile, who was 33 in 1944, stayed behind to look after the priest. Her brother Emile was a pupil at a mission school at Cellule in the Auvergne. He had a brief holiday which started on 8 June. When he arrived at Oradour he found his sister was ill so he helped the priest to do the housework and to prepare for Sunday's service. He also agreed to act as server at the Saturday Mass. Bernadette Cordeau's father was doing forced labour in East Prussia. He had been relieved to learn that she and her mother had returned to Oradour, their former home, from Paris where the family had settled when he got a job there.

Bernadette, who was 16, was living with her mother at the home of her grandmother at Les Bordes, a hamlet a short distance to the north-east of Oradour. She went to Oradour to learn dressmaking while her mother worked as secretary to a doctor in Limoges. On 10 June, Madame Cordeau's employer was on call so she had to stay in Limoges overnight. She told Bernadette it would be best in the circumstances if she went to work in Oradour that day. Of all the people in Oradour on the afternoon of 10 June none could have had any idea of the dreadful thing that was about to happen. None could have imagined they would nearly all be dead by sunset.

Yet those who had seen the SS activity in Saint-Junien may well have been apprehensve. One of them was Denise Bardet, a teacher at the girls' school whose 24th birthday was on that fatal Saturday. She was engaged to a young Limoges man and her brother was at the teacher training college in the city. Denise had accompanied some of her pupils to Saint-Junien the day before

Schoolchildren pictured about 1932. Many of them may have been among the victims of the massacre as adults.

The *Champ de Foire* before the destruction. The communal well confirms that there was no piped water.

Denise Bardet (24 that day) who died in the church with her pupils clinging to her.

and heard of the brutal behaviour of the SS from the townsfolk and of their atrocities in other parts of the region. Saint-Junien had been invaded by an SS unit after the blowing up of a railway viaduct near the town by the maquis.

Denise did not actually witness any brutality but she saw the armed soldiers, who imparted a sense of power and evil, and felt a sense of relief when she and her charges returned to Oradour on the bus with its charcoal burning stove at the rear which provided gas for the motor. The feeling of apprehension provoked by the nearness of the SS may still have been with her when she took her place before her pupils after lunch.

Then a strange sound was heard, increasing in volume as the source neared Oradour...

Oradour had not seen any military traffic before and it was therefore with some surprise that the people in the streets, particularly those at the lower end of the village, heard the rumble of heavy vehicles approaching from the direction of Limoges. The people in the hotels and restaurants were too absorbed in taking their coffee and liqueurs, with typical French animated conversation, to notice the sound. It was the same in the schools where the chattering children had not yet been called to order.

Two trainee teachers from the Limoges college had finished their lunch at the Hôtel Milord and walked to the edge of the village where one, who was working at one of the schools, turned back. The other waved and disappeared in the direction of a nearby hamlet. She was the last person to leave Oradour before the SS arrived.

It was exactly 2.15 p.m. when the SS arrived. As with the rest of the operations, everything was carried out to a time schedule. There were eight trucks, two heavy tracked vehicles and a motor-cycle. Five of the vehicles, three trucks and the tracked vehicles, went straight up the main street almost to the end. There, some of the vehicles turned round and went back down to the bridge over the Glane. Both ends of the main street were now blocked while other vehicles moved to seal the other exits.

The soldiers, who quickly jumped down and ran to their appointed posts, numbered between 150 and 200. They were young men of between 17 and 25 years of age, wearing camouflage tunics and steel helmets with camouflaged canvas covers. Orders were barked by NCOs and there was a rush to surround the entire village. They had orders to shoot anyone who attempted to leave. When the encirclement was complete a white flare was fired.

The people at first watched these manoeuvres with surprise and then with growing disquiet. What on earth was happening? Some thought it was part of the general retreat from the area by the occupation forces, to take part in the battle in the north. Others anticipated a checking of identity papers, nothing more.

Aimé Renaud, one of the few who escaped, said he felt uneasy from the very first and meeting a wine merchant named Denis advised him to go and hide somewhere. Denis said he was not afraid of the Germans. 'They are ordinary men, like us,' he said. 'In any case, I'm old and no longer afraid of anything.'

Mme Clavaud, aged 65, of Champ-de-Bois, was entering Oradour to do some shopping when she was warned by a friend, Mme Puygrenier, that there were Germans in the village.When she saw some of them she thought that, although they looked ferocious, they would not eat her. She was quickly rounded up with the other people.

Marcel Brissaud (17) had just arrived in the village from his home at Les Bordes and, when he saw Germans, was afraid he might be picked up for deportation to Germany for forced labour. The mayor, Doctor Jean Desourteaux, an elderly man with a white beard, and a teacher, Léonard Rousseau, tried to reassure him. There was really no need to be afraid. It was same sort of military manoeuvre which would soon be over.

But Marcel was not convinced. He managed to evade the troops and got back to his home where he took shelter in the loft. He tried to convince his family of the danger if the Germans came their way. When the SS arrived he heard his mother say, 'What on earth can they want us old folk for?' His father had lost a leg in the 1914-18 war. After they had been taken away, he heard the sound of furniture being moved. The soldiers seemed to be emptying cupboards and chests of drawers and he caught a glimpse of them as they were leaving. Some of them were carrying sheets loaded, no doubt, with silver, jewellery and anything else worth looting. When they had gone, he ran to hide in the fields. He later saw his home go up in flames. He was the only survivor of the family.

A Jewish family named Pinède was among the guests at the Hôtel Avril. The parents told their children they knew they would be arrested whatever happened and advised them to hide somewhere. Two girls of 18 and 22 and a boy aged 9 hid themselves under an outside staircase leading to the garden of the hotel. They stayed there until the hotel started to burn.

The youngsters crossed three gardens and were suddenly confronted by an SS trooper who stared at them. The elder girl asked him simply, 'What are we to do?' The soldier, who was probably an Alsatian and understood French, told them to hurry off. They ran through empty houses and gardens and across fields and subsequently found shelter in a château.

A Jewish dentist named Levy, from Limoges, was dining with Mme Jeanne Leroy from Saint-Malo. His wife was in a concentration camp and he had no papers. He fled as soon as he saw Germans in the streets and managed to get out of the village to hide in the fields all day. Mme Leroy stayed, believing there would only be an identity check. She had been obliged to leave her flat in Saint- Malo in 1942 when the Todt Organisation, who built the Germans' West Wall of defence, took over the whole building. She had rented a house near Rennes, but fearing there might be bombing in that area took a friend's advice and moved to the haven of Oradour in April 1944.

The mayor was visited by an SS officer who gave him orders to round up the population. The town crier, Jean Dupierrefiche, set out, accompanied by two soldiers, to beat his drum and announce that everybody must go to the *Champ de Foire* immediately, bringing their identity papers.

Trucks packed with frightened folk, who had been picked up in the neighbourhood, started to arrive. Men were taken from the fields, women and children from the farmhouses and

The church before its destruction.

After the fire.

cottages. Many were weeping.

In fact, the scenes in the countryside around Oradour must have been as dramatic as those in the village.

The Bélivier family lived at a farm at les Brégères, one of the first farms on the road to Limoges. When they saw the SS coming, Mme Bélivier said to her son Marcel, aged 18, 'Hide yourself quickly, petit. They mustn't see you.' He ran into a barn and hid in some hay before escaping into the countryside. He saw his family and some neighbours rounded up and herded like cattle into the village. Later he saw the farm was being destroyed by fire.

The Rouffanche family lived at *La Ferme de l'Etang*. They comprised Jean, a tenant farmer aged 52, his wife Marguerite, aged 47, and their children Jean, Amélie and Andrée. Amélie was a young married woman with a daughter of seven months. The family had just finished their lunch and Jean Rouffanche was preparing to return to his work on the land with his children who helped him run the farm. Marguerite was to stay and look after her grandchild.

Suddenly the SS burst in and ordered them to go to Oradour at once with their identity papers. Amélie put her child in its pram. On the road outside they were joined by neighbours including M and Mme Lamaud who were accompanied by their grandson and granddaughter, elderly mother and maid. Their son and daughter were away at a wedding.

The schools were invaded almost simultaneously. The boys' school, opposite the tram station, had sixty-four pupils. It was conducted by M and Mme Rousseau. The girls' school was in two sections, one in the centre of the village and the other on the road to Les Bordes. The little school for Alsatian refugee children was near the latter. There were 106 girl pupils and twenty-one Alsatians. The girls' teachers were Mlles Bardet, Vincent and Couty, who was standing in for Mme Binet. There was great excitement among the children. It was an unexpected break and promised to be an interesting one. The teachers were apprehensive but tried not to show it. They told some of 'the children they were going to have a group photo taken. The little ones were promised sweets. The children were intrigued by the camouflage uniforms of the SS which they likened to fancy dress.

In one school the teacher had just written the following

sentence on the blackboard for the children to copy:

'Je prends la résolution de ne jamais faire de mal aux autres.'
(I resolve never to do ill to others).

At the little school for the refugees from Alsace-Lorraine, of which M Fernand Gougeon was head, there was quite a different reaction. The children started screaming as soon as they saw the soldiers and could only be made to leave with difficulty.

One of them, Roger Godfrin, aged 8, was the sole survivor of all the schoolchildren in class that afternoon. He said later:

'I am from Lorraine and I knew what the Germans could do. I called to my sisters to run away with me but they only cried and wanted to find our mother. I decided to make a break for it and ran across the yard and through the hedge, where I lost a shoe. A German fired at me so I dropped down and pretended to be dead.

'As soon as all seemed quiet I got up and ran towards the river. The grass was high and I was afraid there might be snakes there. Then I saw something move and thought it was a rabbit, but it was a dog which I called Bobby.

'When I reached the river, which was shallow and narrow at that spot, I waded to the other bank and lay down behind a tree. I heard machine gun fire and looking through the grass I saw that the dog had been killed. I must have fainted then. A roadman found me and carried me to the Laplaud Manor.'

He learned later that all the other members of his family had perished.

At 2.45 the round-up was almost complete. Tension and fear were mounting among the hundreds of people assembled on the village green, surrounded by armed soldiers. Some of them clutched their identity papers. Others had not been given time to collect theirs and feared the consequences. Some mothers carried babies in their arms, others pushed prams. Many babies, woken from their siesta, were fretful. A mother who had left her baby asleep at home was told to go and fetch it. Many women were crying and their husbands were trying to reassure them. The baker Boucholle asked a soldier if he could go back to attend to some pastry in his oven. The reply was, 'Don't worry. We'll take care of it.'

As the schoolchildren came into the square, the clack of their little sabots contrasted with the heavy tread of their threatening escort.

Doctor Jacques Desourteaux arriving back in the village after completing a round of patients in the neighbourhood, was ordered to leave his car and join the other men.

The mayor left the *mairie* accompanied by Messrs Jean Roumy President of the Legion, Montazeau a solicitor, Pascaud a pharmacist, with a number of other tradespeople, the priest and some of the teachers. The mayor had failed to find his son Etienne, who was the town clerk and was rounded up with other people. His other sons were Jacques (the doctor), Emile and Hubert. Hubert, a garage proprietor, was the only survivor.

When they arrived at the *Champ de Foire*, the mayor was confronted by an officer whose words, translated by an Alsatian, were overheard by Robert Hébras, one of the other survivors. The mayor was told, 'We are going to carry out a search of all the houses, but first you must nominate five hostages.'

The mayor, preserving his dignity, said, 'Speaking on behalf of the people, there is no one I can select from them, but if anyone is to be held responsible for any sort of act, I name myself. If you insist on others, you must take my sons.'

He was then escorted away from the scene for a while, during which it was reported that he was told that a German officer was believed to a captive in the village and unless he was produced all the men would be shot. He said he knew nothing of such a prisoner and was taken back to the *Champ de Foire*.

Orders were then given for the men to be separated from the women and children. The separation was carried out with much shoving and shouting by the soldiers. Women who clung to their husbands and sons were forcibly separated.

As soon as the operation was completed, the women and children were herded out of the square on their way to the church.

An unlucky party of young cyclists, five boys and a girl, were seen to arrive at the *Champ de Foire* shortly after the round-up was completed. They were pushing their bicycles and were accompanied by a soldier. They were subsequently lined up against the wall of the forge at the entrance to the square and mown down by a machine-gun.

Another survivor, Jean-Marcel Darthout, said the men were made to sit in three rows facing the houses and forbidden to look round. However, he risked a glance and saw the pitiful party leaving the square.

'Many of the women were weeping,' he said. 'Some were on the verge of collapse and had to be supported by others. I saw my wife for the last time as they turned into the street and disappeared from view. She was in tears.'

The men were addressed by one of the officers. He spoke loudly in German, pausing between sentences for translation. He said there were secret stores of arms and ammunition for 'terrorists' in the village and they would be found. Anyone who knew of the existence of weapons of any sort was advised to speak up immediately. Jean Lamaud, a farmer, said he had a 6 mm carbine and explained that this was permitted by the police. The officer ignored him.

The men were then divided into six groups with between thirty and seventy in each. The major and his son, Doctor Jacques Desourteaux, headed two of these. Each group was then escorted to a different place – the warehouse of M Denis, the Desourteaux garage, the Laudy, Milord and Bouchoule barns and the Beaulieu smithy. On arrival the men were ordered to carry certain encumbrances outside to make more room inside. Carts had to be wheeled out of the Laudy barn.

The SS set up machine-guns on tripods at the entrance to each building and the young soldiers chatted and laughed while they seemed to be waiting for further orders.

The men were tense and some were terrified. But they were relieved to know that their womenfolk and children were safe in the church. They hoped they would released as soon as the search of the buildings had been completed. They feared that someone might have a cache of arms, in which case the person concerned might be deported. But it should not affect the others who had no connection with a maquis group. The hostages might be taken to Limoges and put in the hands of the Gestapo, but the eventuality was unlikely.

Of all the men detained, about 190 in all, only five survived. They were all in the same place, the Laudy barn in the Rue du Cimetière. Their story reveals what must have happened in the other places.

Yvon Roby, an 18 year old postman, said his party numbered just over sixty and when they arrived at the barn they were compelled to remove farm carts before they grouped inside. The soldiers fingered the machine-guns while they chatted and one distributed sugar lumps to the others.

Oradour at that moment held its breath. The women and children crammed in the church listened apprehensively. The men facing the machine-guns listened for any sound which might be comforting. A loudspeaker on a van near the Glane bridge seemed to be emitting orders to the soldiers.

The church clock whirred and struck 3.30. Almost immediately a burst of machine-gun fire was heard. It was a signal. The executioners opened fire, howling as they sprayed bullets around.

Roby dropped to the ground the instant he realised what was happening. He lay on his stomach, protecting his head with his arms. Bullets ricocheted from the wall behind him and he was almost choked with dust. Men had fallen all around him. Some seemed to have been killed instantly but many were only wounded and cried for their wives and mothers.

The fusillade stopped. Spasmodic revolver shots followed, punctuated by groans. Roby realised that the soldiers were finishing off anyone who seemed to be still alive.

'I waited petrified for the bullet that would kill me,' he said, 'but they must have thought I was dead. My left arm was numb. I had been wounded in the elbow. All about me the moaning

The Laudy-Monnier barn shortly after the fire. Five men escaped through the hole in the door at the back.

was stopping. There were fewer shots. Eventually the shooting ceased.'

The soldiers piled faggots, straw, hurdles, ladders and anything else that was combustible on top of the bodies. Then they withdrew. Roby heard what seemed to be a radio playing in the street. There was a German voice followed by martial music.

Roby realised that after all he was not the only one left alive. Under the mass of ladders, hurdles, faggots and straw someone repeatedly asked if there was anyone else alive. One voice replied, then another and another.

Among those who recognised each other were Joseph, a boy apprentice at the barber's shop, Jules Santrot, a tailor, Marcel Brissaud, wheelwright and Poutaraud, a garage proprietor. They had all been wounded, some badly. Poutaraud managed to crawl out from the bodies of the dead and rushed into the street. He was shot as he tried to get through a hedge. Santrot and Brissaud had their legs smashed by bullets and one of them had been hit in the stomach. It appeared that some of the firing had been deliberately aimed low to cripple the victims. But they may have been hit by ricochets.

There was the sound of laughter in the house next door, the home of M Villatte.

The soldiers suddenly returned and set fire to the straw which quickly ignited the other material. As the flames spread, Roby realised he was in danger of being burnt alive.

'I tried to move', he said, 'but the weight of the bodies made it difficult and because of my wound I couldn't use my left arm. However, after a desperate struggle I got free and stood up. I expected to be shot. But the brutes had left.'

The flames and smoke drove him against the wall and he could hardly breathe. Then he saw a panel was missing in the door at the back and managed to squeeze through.

He sought shelter in an adjacent barn where, to his surprise and delight, he found four other survivors. They were Messrs Broussaudier, Darthout, Borie and Hébras.

Three of them hid behind some faggots. Roby sought shelter under a pile of straw and beans. Darthout had been hit in both legs and was bleeding profusely. He begged Roby to find a hiding place for him. Roby dragged him under his cover. Hébras had sustained a head wound and a bullet had

penetrated his right forearm.

They lay there, hardly daring to move, while they listened to the sounds outside.

Suddenly a soldier entered the barn. They held their breaths. A match was struck and they realised he had set fire to the straw. The flames were soon scorching Roby's feet and the smoke almost choked him. In a desperate moment he raised his head. The soldier had gone. The five men came out of their hiding places, and quickly left the barn, dodging the mounting flames. Darthout could barely walk and had to be helped by the others.

They hugged the walls of buildings, seeking another place to hide. Then, hearing German voices, they decided to separate. Roby and Broussaudier made their way to the cemetery, crossing gardens, while the other three sought shelter in a large rabbit house, listening to the frightful sounds outside.

There was an appalling outburst of screaming somewhere lower down the village. The voices were of women and they feared the worst. Later they heard the roar and crackle of big fires nearby. They had to leave the rabbit house when the roof caught fire. They made their way cautiously to the cemetery, fearing they might be spotted and thankful for the smoke screen of the burning buildings. They crossed the cemetery into the open country and eventually found shelter in a thicket. Their movement had been slow and painful, particularly for Darthout who needed help all the way. They were joined by the two who had preceded them.

'We embraced each other fervently,' said Roby. 'So intense was our relief.'

Jean-Marcel Darthout said one of his friends, an Alsatian, remarked as they were being herded into the barn, 'Look out! They are going to kill us!' I told him it couldn't be true, but he insisted, 'Yes, yes! It's true! I heard what one soldier said to another.'

Darthout said he was hit in the calves during the first fusillade and suffered further wounds in his thighs. He believed the soldiers fired low at first so that they would be crippled and could not escape the flames. But why then did the killers clamber over the bodies finishing off anyone who still seemed to be alive?

Just before the killers opened fire Darthout's friend Aliotti asked him if he was going fishing that day. After the fusillade, Darthout was covered with the blood of men who fell on him. He tentatively moved his hand and felt it grasped by another. It was Aliotti who whispered that both his legs were broken. Duquerroix, a gamekeeper, also said his legs were broken.

One of the wounded lifted his head and whispered that the soldiers had gone. They could be heard moving about and talking in the street. Aliotti called the names of his wife and children and bade his friends goodbye.

When the soldiers lit the pyre Darthout's hair caught fire and he had to beat it out with his hands. While he was struggling to free himself he was badly burned on the shoulder. As he dragged himself from the flames he realised from the cries that several of the men were being burned alive. But in his crippled state he could do nothing to help them. He found that one of the panels in the door at the rear had been broken and he crawled painfully through the gap.

Robert Hébras said they were shut in the barn for a while after they had removed the carts. When the doors were opened again they hoped they were going to be liberated. However, they were ordered to clear a patch of floor near the entrance. Then the soldiers brought in two machine-guns and ordered the men to line up in rows facing them.

'I think we knew then that it was all over,' he said.

Some of the men held hands, some folded their arms. One or two turned their backs to the guns. They all went pale. Their mouths dried. The machine-guns were fired in two long bursts. He thought most of the men were hit in the chest.

Exactly what happened in the other places of execution no one, apart from the killers, lived to describe. However, when the salvage teams eventually entered the ruins they found the remains of some women and children among those of the men in a barn on the green facing the church. Women's remains were also found in another barn.

The women locked in the church with the children suffered much physical discomfort, apart from agony of mind. It is estimated that there were 245 of them with 207 children, including six babies under six months, one being only 12 days old, crammed into a building intended for not more than 350. The babies in their prams and pushchairs were put in a side chapel. The schoolchildren who had not been taken in hand by their mothers crowded round their teachers. Many had come from hamlets and farms and their parents were expecting their return that afternoon.

Little Dominique Forest had been separated from his brother but he had his aunt Mme Rousseau to comfort him.

The women were fearful about what might be happening to their menfolk and prayed aloud. A shaft of sunlight shining brightly through the windows gave them a ray of hope.

There was some jostling and irritation when the children cried, but gradually the assembly grew quiet as they listened to the sounds outside.

They heard soldiers shouting. Then suddenly came the sound of machine-guns, firing in bursts near and far. They feared that the worst had happened to the men, Some turned to the consecrated statues, praying on their knees to Sainte Jeanne d'Arc, Notre Dame de Lourdes and Sainte Thérèse. The children howled and clung to the women who tried to comfort them while they themselves trembled and wept. They dreaded to think what they might find when they were released from the church. Despite the inhuman behaviour of their captors, they could not believe that they would violate the sanctity of the church.

The story of what happened next has been told by the sole survivor, Mme Marguerite Rouffanche, the farmer's wife who had been rounded up with the rest of her family.

Mme Rouffanche, the sole survivor of the killing in the church.

She said the main door of the church suddenly burst open and two young soldiers carried in a heavy case from which 'long white cords' trailed. They deposited the case near the altar, lit the cords (fuses) and hastily retreated, locking the door again. The women screamed and backed away from the sinister case. Children were trampled on, chairs overturned. There was an explosion and thick, black, suffocating smoke poured from the case.

(The case is believed to have been packed with smoke-

The window (centre) through which Mme Rouffanche escaped.

The interior of the church shortly after the removal of the human remains. Note the beheaded statue on the left with the entrance to the vestry beyond. The pillar on the right is pitted with the marks of bullets.

The altar area after the church was cleaned up. The vestry has been sealed off.

creating grenades of the type used to winkle out tank crews. It seems to have been specially prepared for the church.)

Everyone crowded into the side chapels and pressed up to the doors and windows. They coughed, choked and screamed as they inhaled the smoke which burned their throats and hurt their eyes.

'The door of the vestry was burst open by some of the panic-stricken women,' said Mme Rouffanche. 'I went through with them and sat on one of the steps. My daughter came to join me.'

She heard gunfire and screaming in the body of the church and the detonation of grenades. The SS had burst in through the main entrance and were firing into the screaming, struggling mass. Then the soldiers noticed that the vestry had been invaded and set about finishing off the women crowded there. Some fired through the windows.

'My daughter was killed by my side. I owe my life to the fact that I shut my eyes and played dead,' said Mme Rouffanche.

When the screaming died down she heard the soldiers gathering chairs and other combustible material to pile on the bodies. She heard them leave when they had started the fire.

As the flames spread it became evident that some of the women, like Mme Rouffanche, had been feigning death. They screamed again as the flames reached them. Most of them could not move, due to their wounds or the pile of bodies on top of them.

'I got to my feet,' said Mme Rouffanche, 'and, concealed by

The confessional in which was found the bodies of two little boys (cousins) who had been shot in the back of the neck.

The high altar with the escape window behind it. The remains of a pram symbolises the slaughter of the babies.

the smoke, slipped behind the altar where there are three windows. I got hold of the step ladder used for lighting the tall candles and managed to reach the centre window, the largest. I still don't know how I managed it, but I squeezed through that window and dropped three metres to the ground.'

Then she realised from a sound above that she was being followed. Henriette Joyeux, aged 23, was holding out her seven months' old baby and pleading with Mme Rouffanche to catch it. She tried, but could not manage to hold it and the child dropped to the ground.

The altar in the side chapel which largely escaped damage.

The infant's screams attracted the attention of some soldiers in the street below and as the two women hurried towards the garden of the presbytery they were fired on. Marguerite Rouffanche was hit five times, four times in her legs. The fifth bullet shattered her right shoulder. However, she managed to drag herself into the garden of the Bardet family, next to the presbytery, where she hid in some rows of peas and tried to cover herself with earth.

Henriette Joyeux, carrying her baby, sought shelter in the privy at the bottom of the presbytery garden, but she had been mortally wounded and died there with her baby whose skull had been fractured. Their bodies were subsequently found in a trench dug by some soldiers who returned to the scene on Monday morning.

The rest of the terrible story could only be pieced together from evidence found by the salvage teams and later by information about people living in the village who, with many visitors, had disappeared and whose remains could not be identified. Many of the children in the church must have been killed by the bullets and grenades. Babies' bodies were found in their prams. In the right transept a large pile of charred human remains was found against a small door which was locked. Yet it appeared that this door had been open at first and two women and eight children had got out that way.

Their bodies were found in the cellar of the presbytery. The wooden confessional in the left transept, which was surprisingly unaffected by the fire, contained the bodies of two boys, cousins aged 12 and 14, who had been shot in the back of the neck. They were upright in the part reserved for the priest and were clutching each other's hands. The vestry, with the remains of the people killed there, had collapsed into the cellar.

There were many isolated killings in and around the village. Bedridden veterans were shot where they lay or allowed to burn to death when their homes were set on fire. One of them, M Giroux, aged 78, who died in his bed, was paralysed. The bodies of several women were found in a well at the Picat farm, on the road to Saint-Junien. The remains of a child were found in the oven of a bakery.

Among the unlucky victims, apart from the five young cyclists who arrived at the time of the round-up, were some workmen on some scaffolding who were shot like pigeons. A young man from Lille, travelling to Toulouse, left the train at Limoges to visit a friend who advised him to spend a few days at Oradour, 'a peaceful little place.' He arrived on the morning of the 10th and managed to find a room at a hotel. Mme Villatte, with her baby Christian aged three months, was staying with her parents-in-law, tobacconists in Oradour, because she feared there might be some aerial bombardment of Limoges. The whole family perished. M Bergeron had come from Saint-Victurnien by bicycle to have some shoes repaired. M Tournier, a music teacher in Limoges, had come to give a lesson.

M. Jules Renaudin who, with his wife, was employed by the Vicomtesse de Saint-Venant at Laplaud Manor, insisted on going into the village after the shooting had started. He was warned of the danger but went to his death saying he must get his tobacco ration and would pick up his seven year old daughter Bernadette who was one of the pupils at the Lorraine School.

There were some miraculous escapes. M Hubert Desourteaux, garage proprietor, a son of the mayor, was a prisoner-of-war for two years and didn't trust the Germans. With his brother Etienne, the mayor's secretary, he hid in some bushes in his garden.

Bullets could be heard ricocheting near them and Etienne decided to take shelter in the house. He was shot there and his body was burnt with the house. Hubert crept into the fields at nightfall and was the only survivor of the family. He was unmarried.

Hubert's mechanic, M Aimé Renaud, also escaped. His wife Jeanine ran to the garage to warn him that the Germans were coming. They hid in his employer's yard, behind some bushes and a pile of stones. They listened horrified to the dreadful sounds, the shooting and screaming in the garage, the explosions, the loud German voices and the crackle and roar of the fires as the houses were set ablaze, one after the other.

They did not dare to emerge from their hiding place until late at night when Mme Renaud almost collided with a soldier. Fortunately he appeared not to notice her. They feared for the safety of their four years old daughter Annie and Mme Renaud's mother, who both died in the church. Together they managed to get out of the burning village and across the river to try to find M Renaud's parents.

Hippolyte Senon, a young man, had cycled out of Oradour

Wrecked cars in the garage near the church.

just before it was surrounded. He went to several farms and hamlets warning people not to go to Oradour. One of the places he visited was the mill on the Glane where the miller's young wife was terrified for the safety of her husband. He had insisted on going into the village on his bicycle, waving a white handkerchief.

She joined the other women, including the mothers of the children at school in the village, to watch with mounting horror and fear the appalling sight of the houses catching fire, one after the other.

A tenant farmer named Gaudy left one of the cottages near the Laplaud Manor to go and find his three children who were at school. He was pulled up short on the road by the sound of machine-gun fire and screaming.

One frantic mother, fearful for the fate of her four children, actually succeeded in getting in and out of the village during the occupation. She was Mme Démery whose children, André (13), Henri (12), Ernest (11) and Marcelle (10), had been taken to the church when she arrived.

Accompanied by a neighbour, she reached the children's school. They heard shooting and screaming lower down the village but saw no soldiers. Frantic with fear, they burst into the school. Mme Démery found her boys' caps and satchels but the school was empty of any living soul.

Another parent who got in and out during the occupation was M. Deschamps, a farm worker at La Fauvette. He thought the woods near the village were on fire and as his four daughters, Claudine (13), Renée (10), Huguette (7), and Maryse (6), had not returned from school he decided to go to the village to see what had happened.

He entered Oradour at the upper end which was sparsely guarded and was surprised to find that the main street was deserted. The doors of the houses were open but there was not a soul in sight. He went into the boys' school and found it strangely empty. He was on his way down to the girls' school when he spotted armed soldiers and decided to return home. He told his wife he thought all the people had been evacuated. The bodies of their daughters were among those which were never identified.

At the Laplaud Manor, Mme Forest became very alarmed when she heard the shooting and screaming which carried a long way. Why had not Michel returned with little Dominique? If there had been any danger they would have come back, bringing her father with them. Accompanied by Doctor and Mme Gaudois, who were also staying at the manor, she walked down the drive to the edge of the woods where they had a view of Oradour. They also thought there was a forest fire on the other side of the village.

'If there is any danger to the village,' they assured each other, 'the people will have been evacuated.'

Among the lucky people who were out of the village that afternoon were Mme Montazeaud, whose husband Pierre, a solicitor, was among the victims, Daniel Senon, a postman who was delivering letters outside Oradour, and M Desvignes, butcher, who had gone to a fair at Saint-Victurien. The Desvignes family perished.

It was around 6 p.m., when the village was burning fiercely that Marie-Léon Foussat, the miller, cautiously approached the

The well at the Picat farm in which bodies were found.

outskirts waving a white handkerchief. A soldier saw him and shot him.

A small maintenance tram from Limoges bearing company employees, stopped before crossing the bridge over the Glane and the driver, M Chalard, got out to see what was happening. He was shot as he crossed the bridge and his body was thrown into the river. The tram was driven back hurriedly.

Another tram, bearing weekend shoppers arrived an hour later. One can imagine their feelings as the tram slowly approached the burning village. One of the guards on the bridge ordered the driver to stop. No one was allowed to get out while a soldier went off on a bicycle to get orders. He returned with the instructions that everyone bound for Oradour was to get out while the rest were sent back to Limoges.

Twenty-two frightened people were marched to the hamlet Les Bordes where a house was on fire. Another house had been taken over as a command post. They were lined up before a soldier with a machine-gun while papers were checked and the men were separated from the women. A grave for a man killed on the road nearby had been dug.

One of the passengers, Louise Compain, daughter of an Oradour confectioner, who was anxious about her parents, said someone asked a soldier what had happened to the villagers.

'*Tous kaput!*' (All dead!) he answered sharply.

'We thought there had been a fight between the maquis and the Germans,' she said afterwards, but one of them told us, in French, ' We found arms and ammunition in the village, so we blew up everything and burnt the place.' The soldier added, 'Above all, don't say anything when the officer arrives.'

Louise said most of the soldiers were laughing and chatting as if they had enjoyed what they had been doing. However, she noticed one young soldier sitting on a stone and wiping his eyes with the sleeve of his uniform. He may have been weeping or his eyes could have been affected by the smoke from the burning buildings.

After about two hours the soldiers encircled the terrified people, pointing their guns at them while there was a conversation between an officer and an NCO. Then to their immense relief the people were told they could go. But they were forbidden to enter Oradour. As they hurriedly moved off, one of the soldiers shouted,

'You can consider yourselves lucky!'

And they didn't know until later just how lucky they were. A soldier had noticed from her papers that one of the girls lived a few kilometres from the village and offered her a bicycle he had stolen during the looting.

Among the 'lucky people' was M Pallier, a railway engineer from Paris. He had intended to visit his wife and two children who had been moved to Oradour to escape a possible bombardment of the capital. Travelling in a chauffeur-driven car, he intended to spend Saturday night with his family.

When they were about four kilometres from the village they met a truck and half-tracked vehicle carrying in all about fifty soldiers. They were

The remains of the post office.

ordered to get out and stand in a ditch while a minute examination was made of their papers. Pallier could speak German and conversed with an officer who asked if he was from Oradour. When he said 'no' he was allowed to carry on. Sundry objects which had been removed from the car were replaced.

They soon saw a huge cloud of smoke arising from the direction of the village and when they came within sight of it they realised to their horror that it was an immense brazier. About 300 metres from the entrance they were stopped by five or six soldiers armed with light machine-guns. They were ordered to get out with their hands raised. They were frisked and their papers were again examined. Pallier explained that he had been given permission by an officer to go to Oradour. He and his chauffeur were ordered not to move and they were eventually ordered to join the evicted tram passengers.

When the tram passengers were released, Pallier was invited by one of the men, whom he knew, to spend the night at his home at Les Bordes. His wife told them that when the Germans arrived she was ordered to prepare a meal for an officer. While she was doing this, one of the soldiers said their mission was to sack and burn Oradour because a much-decorated officer had been the victim of a terrorist attack a short distance away.

The next morning Pallier went with five or six other men to explore the ruins in the hope of finding their missing families. They were utterly shocked by what they saw and had gone right through the ruins and out of the other side when they suddenly came face-to-face with a German patrol. Pallier was recognised by one of the Germans who had stopped his car the previous day. However there was the usual identity check and they were asked if they had been in the village. They said they hadn't yet but intended to if it was allowed. An NCO told them to get away as far as possible or they would be shot.

Pallier and his friend skirted the ruins to return to Les Bordes where they were told that the women and children had been evacuated by the Germans to the hamlet of Maférat before they set fire to the place.

An 80 year old man, Martial Litaud, who had taken shelter in a rabbit hutch during the massacre said he had been back into the ruins and could assure them that there were no more Germans there. So a party of men risked going right through to make their way to Maférat, only to discover that the rumour was false.

M Crémoux, a repatriated prisoner-of-war, managed to get out just before the village was surrounded. For a while he hid in some bushes by the river but got into the water when he heard some soldiers approaching. He was lying in the shadow of the bank when two soldiers, speaking French, passed by. He heard one say, 'I killed twenty-six of them,' as if he had been bagging rabbits.

Armand Senon, aged 20, whose home overlooked the *Champ de Foire*, stayed in his bedroom during the round-up. He was the only survivor of a family of thirteen. He had sustained a broken leg playing football and had it in a plaster cast. He saw the comings and goings of the SS, looking for anyone who might have been overlooked. They shone powerful torches into the windows and one beam touched his plaster cast.

Senon heard the fusillades after the men had been marched off. He witnessed the killing of the six young cyclists outside the Beaubreuil forge. One of them screamed, '*Vive la France!*' before he died. Realising that escape was imperative, he limped downstairs went out by the back door and hid in the garden until nightfall. He heard his home being looted and watched its destruction by fire.

Peering through the undergrowth during the afternoon he saw soldiers firing at people who had escaped the round-up. In fact, they seemed to be firing at everything that moved, including cats, dogs and poultry.

'One of the bastards, a red-headed fellow, crouched down within a few feet of where I was hiding to relieve himself,' he said. 'For one mad moment I thought of braining him with my walking stick.'

The shell of the school for the little Alsatian refugee children from which Roger Godfrin escaped while the others were taken to the *Champ de Foire*.

A neighbour, Maurice Machefer, also escaped but his wife failed to follow him and was taken to the church.

One entire family, together with a woman friend, had an amazing escape. They decided to stay indoors when the order for the assembly was given. A soldier burst in and shoved the two women and two children into the street, ordering them to go to the Champ de Foire. The father, hidden in a bedroom, thought he had been overlooked but another soldier found him and he was made to join the rest of the family in the street.

However, for some reason or other their escort was momentarily distracted and they all managed to slip away and hide in the undergrowth at the back of the house. Later they got away into the woods.

Young Robert Besson hid between two low walls covered with ivy and lay there for eight hours.

A woman named Blanche Taillander also had a remarkable escape. When the SS burst into the house where she was having lunch with a woman friend, they shot her friend and spared her because she pleaded that she came from Paris and was able to prove it by her identity card.

At about 7 o'clock when the firing had died down, Professor Forest, frantic with worry about his two sons, approached the guard at the lower end of the village. He started to talk in German then lapsed into French which the soldier understood.

Ruins of the boys' school.

He was an Alsatian.

As they stood near the burning church where the remains of the women and children were settling into a charred mass, the soldier said all the women and children had gone into the woods and were safe. The professor returned to Laplaud.

That night, while the other Forest children slept, their parents sat on Dominique's empty bed, sleepless and worried.

At Orbagnac, Mme Catherine Lévêque was also frightened. Her daughter Yvonne had gone to Oradour during the afternoon to get some yeast for her mother to make a meat pie. Yvonne had been accompanied by a friend, Marcelle Ratier. Neither had returned. At 3 a.m. Madame Lévêque suddenly screamed, 'We'll never have our child back! I see a pile of charred bones!'

Her husband decided to go into Oradour while it was still dark. He circled the village and eventually ventured into the main street. He got a terrible impression of death everywhere and returned without hope of ever seeing his daughter alive again.

At 5 a.m., Professor Forest returned to Oradour. He asked a sentry in German 'Where are the children?' This time he got the blunt reply, 'They are all dead,' and he was shoved away at gunpoint. As he walked dejectedly up the drive at Laplaud he heard his wife screaming.

Later they received the news of the escape of Aimé and Jeanine Renaud who were their cousins. They hurried to the house at La Plaine where, they were told the Renauds had gone. But they received no comforting news from them.

So Professor Forest returned to the village for the third time. As he crossed the river bridge the smoke and stench blowing his way brought tears to his eyes. This time he persuaded the guard to take him to an officer who shouted that he knew nothing about the children and advised him to get out of the place or he'd be treated like a terrorist.

The whole neighbourhood was lit by the fire as darkness fell. The flames reached their highest when the church was engulfed and there was an enormous clang as the bells crashed down. The fire was visible at Saint-Junien and Limoges.

The first parent to get into the ruined church was a farmer named Hyvernaud. His two sons, Marcel (12) and André (6), had not returned home and at 4.30 a.m. he decided to investigate. As if by instinct, he went straight to the church. Among the blackened, stinking human remains he recognised the half-burnt body of André. His throat had been severed and one leg was broken and twisted back. He still wore one of his sabots. Hyvernaud returned to his farm at Le Breuil, two kilometres north-east of Oradour, and told his wife what he had found.

They both returned to the church with some sheets. They couldn't recognise Marcel among the other remains so they wrapped up what was left of André and took him home. They buried him in the farmyard.

During his search for his other son, Hyvernaud had looked behind the altar where he found the remains of about twenty small children. They appeared to have been put there in the hope that they would be safe. He saw a number of dead babies in their prams.

All the houses were looted and valuables, radios, drink and food were loaded into trucks. As each house was cleared the soldiers doused the interiors with petrol and ignited them. However, one building, La Maison Dupic, a draper's shop, was not destroyed with the rest. It was emptied of much of its stock, but the SS had a use for it later. It was selected to be a sort of guard post for the night. The rearguard had an orgy there with much drinking and singing. They set fire to the premises when they left at about 11a.m. on Sunday. About twenty-five empty champagne bottles were found near the ruins.

Armand Senon, the escapee with the broken leg, heard the last of the trucks leave but dared not leave his hiding place until several hours later. When he cautiously limped into the ruins he almost immediately came upon the body of Pierre-Henri Poutaraud, the garagist who survived the shooting in the Laudy barn. He had been shot in back and was halfway through a fence. The first living soul he met was M Devignes, the butcher, who told him that everyone had been killed and their bodies burnt. He was in tears. Senon searched in vain for any trace of his family.

A few other people made a cautious appearance after the SS had left, staring in horror at the ruins. The transformation of a peaceful, picturesque village into a smoking, stinking ruin was shocking in itself without investigation of what the ruins contained. Certain buildings were recognisable because their signs were still legible, if charred: Hôtel Milord, Hôtel Beaubreuil, Restaurant Dagoury, Café de Chêne, Boulangerie and Boucherie, among others. But they bore no resemblance to the busy, populated places of the previous day.

A few horses and some cattle roamed the streets looking for their stables and barns. Dogs sniffed among the ruins for their masters, whining and shivering. Most of the cats seemed to have taken refuge in a house on the outskirts which had been spared and were howling to be fed. Swallows darted about distraught because their nests had been burnt. Poultry and rabbits foraged in the gardens.

That same day, anxious families and friends went to the office of the Gestapo in the Champ de Juillet, Limoges, to ask for news of people and children who had been in Oradour. The Germans refused to see them but some policemen who were guarding the building said: 'We can't give you any details but one thing is clear – everyone has perished.'

Among the people who entered the ruins later that day were M Hubert Desourteaux and M Lévignac who still hoped to find his two sons. Léviginac ventured into the ruined church and soon emerged shocked and unbelieving. Then he heard a faint cry and traced the source to the garden of the Bardet family where he found what he thought was a negress lying between the rows of peas. It was Marguerite Rouffanche who had covered herself with earth.

She was so distraught that she begged her rescuers to throw her in the river. She had been lying there for nearly twenty-four hours. They put her in a barrow and took her to Laplaud Manor. She was covered with a mixture of blood and soil. She could hardly speak but her rescuers could just distinguish a repeated sentence, 'All the women and children where burned in the church...'

At the manor, Doctor Gaudois cut away her clothing and did his best to clean her up. He realised that her five bullet wounds needed urgent attention but he had no facilities. However, they kept her at the manor overnight. The next morning they took her to the station at Saint-Victurnien where they managed to get on a goods train for Limoges. On their way to the hospital they were stopped by a German soldier who was curious about their patient. However they managed to convince him that she had fallen from a hay loft.

A Limoges journalist, Pierre Poitevin, subsequently visited Marguerite Rouffanche in hospital with a friend of hers. She had refused to see anyone, particularly journalists, except a few friends and relatives. Poitevin did not reveal his identity and she did not query it.

She spoke in a low voice about the terrible scenes in the church. She said her two daughters, Andrée Rouffanche, (21), and Mme Amélie Peyroux (23), had gone into the vestry with her. In the rush Amélie had dropped her baby. She found him shortly before they were both killed by bullets. Andrée had been killed at her side and she had also lost her husband and her son Jean (19).

Mme Rouffanche said she was sorry she had been unable to catch Henriette Joyeux's baby when she dropped it from the church window. She told how she tried to cover herself with earth while she lay among the peas. Her wounds were very painful and she suffered greatly from thirst. She managed to clutch a few handfuls of peas and sucked them to alleviate her thirst.

Early on Sunday morning she heard men's voices. She slowly turned her head and saw some soldiers milking a cow a short distance away. When they moved away she tried to crawl further into the undergrowth but her wounds made it impossible. She wished she could crawl down to the Glane and die there. But she could not move.

CHAPTER THREE

The Dreadful Toll

The destruction of Oradour involved 254 buildings of which 123 were houses. When the list of the dead came to be drawn up it was established that the residents, together with the refugees, totalled 393. People who were brought in from the countryside totalled 167. There were thirty-three people from Limoges and forty-three from other places. Six others were subsequently added to the list as it turned out that they had disappeared and must have been in Oradour at the time.

One man whose name was not listed was Lieutenant Knug of the SS. He was killed when a stone from the church steeple hit him as it collapsed. His family were told that he had been killed in action, fighting for the Führer and Fatherland.

After the sacking of the village the SS travelled to the village of Nieul, about nine and a half kilomeres away, where billets for the night had been arranged. Someone who saw them pass said some of them were singing to an accordion. Residents of Nieul described how they arrived in a state of excitement. They spread out in the streets, shouting to each other. Some appeared to be drunk. Most of the soldiers were billeted in the village school. After washing off their grime in the children's toilets they drank their looted liquor and settled down for the night in the children's classrooms. The officers spent the night in a private house.

The following day, Sunday 11 June, the soldiers made meals from poultry they had stolen. Some of them fooled around in the playground with two bicycles until they smashed them. These were identified as belonging to Oradour people, as also was a motor-cycle found in a park pond. One soldier was seen at the ground floor window of a house distributing banknotes from two canteens. Two French truck drivers named Démery and Nadaud, who had been commissioned to help with the transport of the battalion's accoutrements from Saint-Junien, said an Alsatian told them, 'We have just carried out quite a job. We have killed all the people of Oradour and burnt them in the church.'

The last of the SS to leave Oradour on Sunday morning, after the burning of the Maison Dupic, were seen en route for Nieul by Hubert Desourteaux. Their trucks were loaded with loot and they were towing a car which he recognised as the property of one of his customers. The rope snapped and the car crashed into a pylon. The man at the wheel was badly hurt. The others put him in a truck, together with the loot from the car and carried on. The SS in Nieul spent much of Sunday in a state of readiness seated in the trucks. They were joined by other companies of the battalion.

On the morning of the 12th a party of soldiers arrived at the ruins. Their orders were apparently to try to conceal some of the evidence of the massacre. People who had been searching for their families fled in fear while animals roaming about were shot. The men were equipped with spades and dug trenches behind the barns and warehouses where the men had been killed. They also dug a large trench near the church. Into these trenches they threw the remains of as many bodies as they would hold and flattened the earth on top. The burial of M Dupic, in his own garden, was so rudimentary that one of his hands was above ground. The bodies of the two women and eight children who were shot in the cellar of the presbytery were covered with earth and stones and bullet-riddled prams were thrown on top. The soldiers also buried a number of isolated corpses on the outskirts of the village. They left the scene at about mid-day, after firing a burst from their machine-guns. They were seen travelling towards Limoges.

For a while the Germans put a guard on the ruins and forbade anyone to enter. Some officers paid a visit and after a brief inspection left with some poultry.

Later that day, 12 June, the first official visitor, the prefect of Rochechouart, went through the ruins and described what he had seen to the prefect of Limoges, M Freund-Valade. The latter made a personal visit the following day, accompanied by the Bishop of Limoges, Mgr Rastouil. The bishop was so shocked by what they found in the church that he burst into tears and nearly fainted. In a letter to the Vichy government, in which he deplored the massacre, the prefect wrote:

'In the church we found the remains of many human beings who had been burned. The floor was littered with empty cases of bullets bearing the maker's mark S.T.K.A.M. and the walls bore numerous bullet holes at the height of a human being. Outside

the church the earth had recently been moved. The remains of
women and children had been buried there by German soldiers.
There was a pile of charred clothing belonging to children.'

The prefect said a few people had managed to get into the ruins
on the Sunday afternoon and some of them saw the burnt and
broken bodies in the church.

'One witness,' he wrote, 'swore he had seen the body of a
mother clutching an infant in her arms before the altar, there
was also the body of a little child, its hands joined in prayer.'

The prefect appealed to the Vichy government to protest in
the strongest terms to the German government about 'the
appalling nature of such reprisals, the widespread emotion they
had aroused and the terror the people were experiencing.'

On the afternoon of the 14th, Commander de Praingy,
assistant director of the Défense Passive, visited the ruins,
accompanied Doctor Bapt, the medical officer of health, his
deputy Doctor Benech, and twenty members of the Red Cross
emergency service. They were there to assess the extent of the
salvage work. Commander de Praingy subsequently phoned
the prefect to ask for a team composed of members of the Red
Cross, the *Jeunesse Secours* (a young people's aid association)
and of the *Equipes Nationales* to accompany him to Oradour the
next day. He dictated a list of the equipment needed.

On Thursday morning, the 15th, a team of 149 people,

A recovery team pulling a cart load of remains to the burial pit.

including a number of young seminarists, left Limoges by tram. They carried disinfectants, face masks, rubber gloves and shovels. Stretchers and coffins were in a trailer attached to the tram. There was also some food for the workers, who expected to be there all day.

They carried a permit issued by General Gleiniger, the *Wehrmacht* officer in charge of the Limoges district, which read:

PERMIT

Limoges 14.6.44

The army headquarters gives permission today and on succeeding days for members of the French sanitary service (Red Cross), under the leadership of Dr Bapt (M.O.H. for the dept of Haute-Vienne), together with his assistant Dr Benech, to travel from Limoges to Oradour-sur-Glane to carry out urgent sanitary and clearing work.

This permit is valid until 22.6.44 when it must be returned to these headquarters.

Signed : The Commandant,
Gleiniger
Major-General

The odd part about this was the insistance that the document should be returned in eight days' time, the apparent assumption being that the work would then be completed.

Gleiniger is said to have expressed profound shock when he heard of the destruction of the village and its people and realised that sanitary precautions were essential to prevent an outbreak of disease. The salvage team soaked their face masks with eucalyptus oil as the stench had become almost unbearable. During a rest period they tried to eat some of the food but they had no appetite.

In the streets they found the wrecks of two cars, one being that of Doctor Desourteaux, and the bicycles belonging to the young visitors who had been shot in front of the smithy. An odd discovery was a number of cardboard boxes bearing the name of the American munitions firm Winchester. They seemed to have been deliberately placed in the ruins when the fires were out. Surely the Germans weren't so stupid as to think such evidence might lead people to think there was an American connection with the massacre?

Dead farm animals had been burnt or buried. In the ruins of one farm there were thirty dead sheep. Surviving cows bellowed to be milked. Working among the human debris, the salvage team felt that the accusation that the SS had fired low at first, to cripple their victims, might be correct as the legs of many corpses were shattered. In Russia, shooting below the waist was the order given to some firing squads, in order to inflict painful wounds before the final despatch of the victims.

In the church some of the religious emblems had been smashed and a war memorial was riddled with bullets. But the statues of Notre Dame de Lourdes and Sainte Thérèse were unscathed. Also intact were the recently resilvered crucifix just outside the church and, surprisingly, a wooden cross attached to a gutted house opposite. Pickaxes had to be used in the Chapelle Sainte-Anne as the mass of remains was as hard as cement.

Commander de Praingy ordered the setting up of barricades at the entrances to the ruins. Sightseers were sent away and only people who had a special reason were allowed to enter. They included some of the bereaved, although every effort was made to dissuade them, in view of the shocking sights they might see. Passes had to be obtained at the temporary *mairie* which had

A burial party, wearing handkerchiefs soaked in eucalyptus to cover the stench, removing charred remains from one of the execution sites.

been set up in a barn at the Bel Air Farm.

There was strict surveillance to prevent looting. Items of value, such as jewellery, gold and silverware which, with a few identity cards had somehow survived the blaze, were collected and taken to the Banque de France in Limoges. Each piece bore a label indicating where it had been found. Odd finds included wallets with banknotes intact (though one had been perforated by a bullet) and numerous clasp knives. Four knives had been opened, as if their owners had been prepared to tackle the raiders. Among the remains of the women were belt buckles, corset stiffeners and lipstick tubes.

A letter stained with blood was addressed to a priest and dated 10 June. It began, 'I am quite well at present and benefiting from the sunshine...' A page of an exercise book belonging to an 11-year-old boy bore a sentence copied from the blackboard, *'Je prends la résolution de ne jamais faire du mal aux autres...'*

On the altar, the tabernacle had been forced open and the sacred vessels removed. A small box containing sacred relics was dug up near the church but the ciborium was never recovered. It had probably been included in the SS loot. The Bishop of Limoges wrote to General Gleiniger. After expressing his horror about the massacre in the church, he wrote, 'It is my duty to find out what happened to the sacred vessels, not so much for their value as for what they contained – the sacred host...' The general expressed his regret and said he was shocked by the whole affair. One of his officers, an Austrian, is said to have remarked, 'It would have been better for Germany to lose another five divisions than to carry the guilt of the massacre of Oradour.'

Doctor Bapt reported that the bodies that could be identified were buried separately, each with its identifying cross. However, the vast majority of the human remains were impossible to identify and would be put in a communal grave.

He had gone to Les Bordes on his bicycle on the 19th when he was told that the Germans had returned to the ruins. He hurried back and found three truckloads of soldiers at the southern entrance. Some of them were in the streets and he saw two of them removing wheels from wrecked cars. He showed his permit and found the salvage team still at work. They told him that the Germans had seized the bicycles used by some of the

Remains laid out for collection.

team and loaded them on the trucks. However they got them back when they convinced the soldiers they were doing an authorised task.

This unexpected return of the Germans added to the terror of the communities in the neighbourhood who had been stunned by the massacre. Fearing further atrocities they left their homes at night to sleep in the woods.

Pierre Poitevin, a Limoges journalist, a member of the MUR *(Mouvements Unis de Résistance)* whose pseudonym was Jean Guiton, had clandestinely visited villages in the Dordogne and Corrèze, where the SS had committed atrocities, and got permission from his editor to visit Oradour on the afternooon of the 19th. Despite a German ban on photographs he took his camera and and had taken a number of pictures of the ruins and the salvage team at work when he was stopped by a German NCO who demanded to see his papers. Fortunately he had pocketed his camera, a folding one, but it made a bulge in his pocket. He had to wait against a wall, guarded by four armed soldiers, while his identity card was examined. He prayed he would not be frisked. Fortunately his card described him as 'an inspector' – as a member of the Resistance this was a safer description than 'journalist'. He said he was working for an insurance company and had come to the village to assess the damage to property. He was also working with the salvage party.

The soldier who interpreted appeared doubtful and it was fortunate that an engineer M Fichot, who had also been questioned, confirmed his identity and they were both released. They hurried to their bicycles only to find they had been loaded on a truck. They had to ask the interpreter to help them to retrieve them. Incidentally, Poitevin buried his reports of the SS atrocities including Oradour, until the liberation. He feared a Gestapo investigation.

When the Gestapo heard there were some survivors they did their utmost to trace them. Fortunately, these stricken people were warned by the Resistance who helped them to find shelter. They also helped them financially. No official monetary help was given until July when clothing and cash were distributed at the temporary *mairie* at the Bel Air farm.

The salvage team worked for five days, digging up and transporting bodies while in constant fear of being interrupted by the Germans and constant danger from falling masonry. On the last day, the last cart, drawn by oxen and covered with flowers and greenery, arrived at the burial pit with its tragic load. A tricolour flag with a black veil was at the front of the vehicle. The unidentified remains of hundreds of people in the pit were covered with quicklime. Before the pit was filled in the salvage team with a number of relatives of the dead gathered round for a committal service conducted by the bishop. Two social workers, Mlles Lacoste and Dumay threw into the pit a beautiful wreath of roses gathered from the gardens of the ruined houses.

Before dispersing, the people held hands and sang *'Ce n'est qu'un au revoir, mes frères'*. Tears flowed and some of the women fainted.

Every possible effort had been made to identify the bodies but most were unrecognisable. However, the body of the mayor dug from a trench was identified. He had been shot in the heart and buried with his briefcase. One report said that the body of the parish priest had been found in the church but this was never confirmed. There were two priests: the Abbé Chapelle, the parish priest and the Abbé Lorich from Alsace-Lorraine. There was also a young seminarist, Emile Neumeyer in village on that fatal afternoon. They all disappeared without trace, although the first two were noticed among the assembly at the *Champ de Foire*.

The remains of the mayor, identified by a briefcase he was holding.

Compiling a provisional list of the dead was difficult because the parish registers and other important documents had been destroyed. Some help was given by the bereaved and outsiders who knew the village and its inhabitants. They walked from one ruin to another naming the people they thought had lived there.

On 6 July, the Bishop of Limoges had told a large congregation in the cathedral what he had seen at Oradour and announced that a memorial service would be held on 21 June at 9.30 a.m. As reference to the massacre in the press was forbidden, the Bishop arranged for the announcement to be made in all the churches. The service was described as 'a memorial to the recent dead.' Without direct reference to the occupying forces, he said 21 June would be a day of mourning, associated with expressions of sympathy for the bereaved and a protest against 'appalling barbarity.'

The German censor in Limoges, Doctor Sahm, called a meeting of local journalists in his office in the Rue Pierre-- Raymond. He first spoke of the new German offensive weapons, *aerodynamic meteorites*' (the V1 and V2) which were being targeted on London and deplored the lack of interest in them shown in the press.

Then he said:

'Gentlemen, I must now speak of a matter which has had a profound effect on me. I refer, of course, to what has happened at Oradour. Please understand that we offer no excuses for what happened and I cannot tell you if the officers concerned will be punished or if they have already been disciplined. But I must stress that the soldiers did not go to Oradour without a reason. The village was full of maquis, in fact it was a maquis stronghold. On 9 June and even on the morning of the 10th they fired on cars carrying officers. The soldiers could therefore claim that they acted in legitimate defence. Concerning what happened in the church, where the women and children were sent for their safety, I must admit that I cannot understand it and we will try to find the reason.'

Then after a pause and without a word of sympathy for the bereaved, Sahm added 'After all, gentlemen, you will appreciate that many more women and children have been killed by RAF bombers than at Oradour.' The journalists listened to this statement in silence. There was another pause then Sahm added, 'I think it would be preferable for you to make no reference to this affair at present.' In the event the newspapers published many death notices placed by the families of the victims, until the Germans put a stop to the practice.

Charred bodies of women and children taken from a trench near the church.

The torso of a woman with her hand clenched, near the body of a little boy.

Human remains on a makeshift stretcher.

From Sahm's statement the journalists were asked to believe that the SS did not make a chance visit to Oradour. They had been ordered to go there. But by whom and what was the real motive for the raid? If there had been any truth in officers being fired on from the village and there had been fatal injuries, impressive funerals with full military honours would have been witnessed.

Attempts were made to keep the people away from the cathedral on the 21st when all the shops and cafés were closed and flags appeared at half-mast. There was a rumour that the bishop had been arrested and that explosives had been placed under the cathedral to be detonated during the service. Before the service, the prefect warned the bishop that nocturnal work had been reported near the cathedral. The police searched the crypt but found nothing. The Bishop went to the cathedral at 9.30 a.m. to find it already full with a large crowd outside.

During the service, the prefect told the Bishop that the police could not assure him there was no danger and advised him to shorten the service. It was later revealed that a man in the pay of the Gestapo had made a noise in a cellar adjacent to the cathedral during the night. It sounded like excavation. The Bishop concluded the service with the words, 'Mes frères, let us say the *De Profundis* for the dead of Oradour-sur-Glane. Let us say a *Pater* and an *Ave* for the families of the victims.'

The next day, Monseigneur Valerio Valeri, the Papal Nuncio at Vichy, sent a letter of protest to Pétain. He expressed his horror at what had happened at Oradour and implored the Marshal to transmit the feelings of the people to the German government. Pétain wrote to Hitler complaining about the campaign of reprisals which, he said, 'would gravely compromise the reconciliation of our two peoples.' There was no reply.

The attitude of the Vichy government was expressed by a spokeman, Xavier Vallat, in a broadcast on the controlled radio on 27 June. He referred to a woman he knew who had died at Oradour, 'The French people are morally responsible for the death of this woman and many others' and went on to explain that if they had not allowed a group of 'bandits' to cause grave unrest or false patriotism the Germans would not have been obliged to inflict punishment on so many people.

On 3 July a representative of the regional office of information asked the Bishop to arrange a memorial service for Philippe Henriot, propaganda minister for the Vichy government, who had been shot by *francs-tireurs* in Paris. The Bishop said such a service could be arranged but he would take

Boxes containing the remains of bodies awaiting collection.

The funeral cortege on the way to the service at the burial pit. The cart, drawn by oxen, was loaded with flowers.

no part in it, in view of the official character of the ceremony.

The following day, two of the leaders of the local militia, a collaborationist force, Messrs Vaugelas and Raybaud, came to tell him that if he still refused to take part in the service it would be considered 'a hostile act' in the eyes of the Vichy government. The Bishop replied that he would not attend, even if it cost him his liberty or even his life. The service took place on 5 July when the Bishop was 'represented' by a *vicaire-général* and there were a few other priests. That evening, Radio Limoges complained in strong terms that a prominent ecclesiastic of Limoges had refused to take part in the memorial service for M Henriot. On 7 July, four policemen came to the Bishop with an order to take him under open arrest to a

The funeral service at the pit which held hundreds of burnt bodies covered with quicklime.

detention centre at Chatroux. Warned of the visit, the Bishop wore his impressive purple habit to welcome them. An inspector first apologised then read the order of arrest, signed by Raybaud, which accused the Bishop of being 'a person dangerous to national defence and public security.' The Bishop refused to move and the policemen left.

Later that day, the same policemen returned with an order to take him by force if necessary. The Bishop replied,

'My dear sirs, you are but little people in reality. You are like us, sons of working folk. I don't want you to act against your conscience or to risk losing your livelihood, so I'll come.'

At Chatroux his guards were polite and even sympathetic. Meanwhile the *Papal Nuncio* called on Pétain's Prime Minister Pierre Laval to protest about the Bishop's arrest which, said, could have 'grave repercussions.' He also told Laval in no uncertain terms what had happened at Oradour. Laval contacted Darnaud, the chief of the militia, and on 22 July an order was given for the Bishop's release. As his car had been taken by the maquis, and the police did not provide transport, the Bishop had to walk back to Limoges, a distance of about seven kilometres. He was greeted with joy and surprise by everyone he met.

On the day of the liberation of Limoges, 21 August, people gathered round the Bishop to talk about the tragedy of Oradour and to thank him for his noble and courageous stand against the Germans and the militia.

There are conflicting accounts about what happened to General Gleiniger, the officer in charge of the Limoges district, who apologised for the massacre, of which he apparently had no prior knowledge. But what is certain is that he died shortly afterwards, either by assassination or suicide.

In September 1994, an article by René Lejeune appeared in a religious magazine under the heading: 'ORADOUR – UN MARTYR DE PLUS.' (Oradour – Another Martyr) Lejeune said his brother was a seminarist at Limoges in 1944 and was among those who helped to inter the bodies of the victims. He spoke of General Gleiniger as a man who tried to save the honour of his people. As soon as he heard of the massacre the general begged the pardon of the prefect of Limoges, on behalf of his fellow countrymen. The *Das Reich* division were furious and accused him of 'sullying the honour of National Socialism in a

General Gleiniger, the officer in charge of the Limoges district, apologised for the massacre.

disgraceful manner.' They ambushed him just outside Limoges and killed him.

The *Bundesarchiv* (German archives) have a report from an NCO stationed at the military headquarters in Limoges, which says, the General was visited by three officers of the *Das Reich* division on Sunday, 11 June. They submitted a report of only three lines stating that there had been resistance to the armed forces at Oradour and the village had been razed to the ground. At that time, the NCO reported, tension between the SS and the Army was at its strongest and the SS officers warned Gleiniger that any sort of trouble between the two could lead to casualties.

Later, the report said, the SS arrested the General at his headquarters and put him in the back of a truck going in convoy towards Guéret. He (the NCO) and several other soldiers joined the convoy. On the way, there was a brief clash with some maquisards. When the shooting was over, the back of the truck carrying the general was opened and it was found that he had shot himself with a light machine-gun clapsed between his knees with the muzzle under his chin. Two or three bullets had pierced his skull. When the convoy reached Guéret, the SS decided to bury Gleiniger in the cemetery, but not in the part reserved for the military dead. They interred him in a rubbish dump and piled discarded and disintegrated wreaths on him. He had been regarded as a traitor.

Bundesarchiv believes this version to be true, though no dates are given. In view of the other information about the General's activities it is apparent that the *Das Reich* division could not have been involved in his death. Apart from the fact that he was

Some of the survivors of the massacre: Front row (from the left) Armand Senon, Mathieu Borie, Daniel Senon, Clement Broussaudier, Joseph Beaubreuil, Robert Besson, Paul Doutre, Martial Machefer. Back row: Yvon Roby, Marcel Darthout (with Glasses), Maurice Beaubreuil, Hubert Desourteaux, Aimé Renaud. In front is Roger Godfrin, the sole survivor of the children, orphaned by the death of the rest of his family.

Roger Godfrin, the boy who ran away from the Alsatian school when the SS arrived to take them to the *Champ de Foire*. His parents, father aged 37 and his mother 35, died in the massacre with their other children, aged 3, 4, 11 and 13. Roger returned to his home town Charly (renamed Charly-Oradour). He was born in 1936 and died in 2001.

reported to have been in Limoges in July, when the *Das Reich* would have been in Normandy, they would not have taken him north-east towards Guéret when their direct route to the battlefield was north, via Poitiers.

In letters to Vichy from the prefect, M. Freund-Valade, dated 15, 16 and 17 June there is mention of contacts with the General. On 15 June the prefect wrote that he went to see Gleiniger on Monday, 12 June, to protest about 'a method of repression that was contrary to all the laws of warfare and had caused horror and indignation throughout the whole region.' It seemed that the General had received incomplete information about what had happened at Oradour and when told expressed his astonisnment and indignation.

On 16 June, the prefect reported that he had been summoned to Gleiniger's headquarters the previous day. The general seemed shocked by the massacre. When the prefect said it disgraced the German Army, Gleiniger agreed and added, 'This action is a crime against the German people and merits the most severe punishment for those who are responsible.'

The prefect said the French people were waiting for an announcement by the German government dissociating themselves from the massacre. He suggested that Gleiniger might ask the government for permission to release a number of local prisoners, including men from the canton of Saint-Junien which included Oradour, as a preliminary gesture of recompense. The prefect said he hoped there would be an inquiry on the spot, under the supervision of the Red Cross. He also hoped Pétain would come to see what had happened and express his sympathy with the bereaved.

He wrote to Vichy again on 17 June about the lack of interest shown by the police. He put this down to the fact that the police chief who he had appointed had been arrested by the militia. He had been replaced by a member of the *Guarde Mobile de Réserve*, appointed by M de Vaugelas, a militia officer. The prefect said that in view of the restriction of movement in Limoges and surroundings he had asked Gleiniger for a pass to allow him to circulate freely in the area for which he was responsible. It was refused.

Gleiniger was regarded by the army and the collaborators as a 'softy.' His tolerant, understanding attitude was illustrated by a notice he placed in the local press and in posters pasted up in various parts of the city. He announced that he had appealed to the Führer for permission to release a number of local prisoners. He offered to provide trucks to help in the transport of fruit and vegetables for the deprived population.

However, no prisoners were released and not only did no trucks appear, but the soldiers actually accelerated their requisition of vehicles for their personal use. In the markets, the soldiers took their pick of the produce with no regard for the needs of the people.

Pierre Poitevin, the Limoges journalist, said the General and his staff did not visit Oradour until 16 July, after which the General disappeared. He heard that he had been killed by his own men. Another version was that he had been wounded in Guéret when he fled with his troops and the Limoges militia towards the east. It seems certain that his arrest and death did not take place until after 16 July. Then who was responsible?

One theory was that he had been removed from his post and transported towards Germany under orders from Himmler. In which case, the SS would have been involved and they would probably have been members of the 19th Regiment of SS Police who were stationed in Limoges, in collaboration with the Gestapo, who would know all about Gleiniger's 'treason'.

CHAPTER FOUR

The Guilty

The massacre was carried out by a detachment of the 3rd Company of the 1st Battalion of the No 4 Panzer-Grenadier Regiment, *Der Führer*, of the 2nd SS Panzer Division, *Das Reich*, commanded by General H B Lammerding

The raid was led by Major Adolf Diekmann, the CO of the battalion, accompanied by Captain Otto Kahn, commanding the 3rd Company, and several other officers. The division was on its way to the Normandy battlefield from the south of France. How these young soldiers (mostly aged between 17 and 25) can have carried out such pitiless slaughter cannot be understood without a study of the SS character and the events that led up to the massacre.

The SS or *Schutzstaffel* (protection squad) was formed as a personal bodyguard for Hitler. In 1929 when he appointed Heinrich Himmler, aged 28, as *Reichsführer* SS, there were about 280 men in it. Himmler was instructed to produce an élite Nazi troop, utterly dependable in all circumstances. In 1933, when Hitler became Chancellor, the ranks of the SS had swollen to about 52,000. They were nominally part of the SA (*Sturmabteilung* or Brownshirts) who numbered 300,000. In 1934, the SA, led by Ernst Röhm, were getting out of hand and demanding a social revolution. Hitler decided to purge them. He used his SS for the notorious assassinations of 30 June 1934, the 'Night of the Long Knives', when Röhm and other SA officers were 'liquidated.'

In the years prior to the war the combat units of the SS were increased in number, not as part of the *Wehrmacht* (Army) but as a standing force at Hitler's disposal. They were subjected to intensive indoctrination, politically and ideologically. The SS were prominent in the occupation of the Sudetenland, Austria and Czechoslovakia. The young soldiers revelled in their physical fitness, which involved strenuous athletics and gruelling

Ernst Röhm, SA Commander. He was murdered, along with many of his officers, by the the SS in the Night of the Long Knives.

A guard of the *Leibstandarte Adolf Hitler*.

trials. One trial involved a recruit digging a hole for himself within a strict time limit before a tank ran over him. There was a cameraderie between officers and men which could never be found in the army.

Many of the officers were of humble origin, far removed from the Prussian aristocrats who still found a place among the élite of the army. Most of them were under 30 and, wearing the most attractive dress uniform in the German armed forces, they found easy conquests among the females. They had their own brothels. Yet despite their lack of intelligence and imagination, the *Waffen* SS (Fighting SS) had no equal among the German forces in the field. They were utterly faithful to their beloved Führer and unafraid to die in carrying out his orders. Their ruthless behaviour with innocent people during the war is unquestionable. They killed men, women and children without qualms, looted and burned whole towns and villages. They were trained to ignore the 'rules' of warfare (the Geneva Convention) and the weak and innocent were just targets for their sophisticated weapons.

Yet they respected brave enemies. A British officer in the ill-fated Arnhem campaign told me that the SS with whom he was engaged in bloody conflict treated their prisoners well, and gathered and tended the British wounded. They were usually courteous to civilians on whom they were billeted and the officers were reported to have shown almost excessive gallantry to their hosts, particularly women. Their devotion to their Führer ensured that their only salute was '*Heil Hitler.*'

In the selection of recruits, intelligence was not an important asset. In the whole of the war there was no high commander in the SS to compare with the top brass of the army. The prime consideration was complete and unquestioning obedience to orders, however insane they might seem, coupled with bravery in battle. The officers' greatest fear was that they might be seen to crack on the battlefield.

Ulrich von Hassell, who was executed in September 1944 for his part in the campaign to remove Hitler, described the SS as having 'an ambiguous psychology'. In them 'two souls lived in strange confusion, – one a barbarian, the soul of the Nazi party, the other a perverted aristocratic soul.' Their blind ideology led to heavy casualties in their ranks. They were taught to be contemptuous of death, their own as well as their adversaries'.

They were judged by the glory of their achievements, whatever their losses might be.

Their losses were so heavy in the great tank battle of Kursk, during the Russian campaign, that their ranks had to be reinforced by men from the occupied countries and even from German prisons, a procedure hitherto inconceivable to this élite force. Their respect for bravery in the field extended to Russian soldiers (who fought with grim determination) but they could still destroy whole Russian towns and villages, and massacre thousands of innocent people. The toll in many places being worse than Oradour's.

With the outbreak of the war, the SS leapt into the attack on Poland with ill-concealed joy and enthusiasm. This was the culmination, the vital test of their training, their ultimate goal.

Complaints about atrocities committed by the SS arose early in the conflict. They usually came from the army. Hitler warned the generals that there would be activities in the conquered territory 'which might not be to their taste,' but they should not interfere. Fifty Jews who had been rounded up in Poland for forced labour were shot by the SS. The army commander in the area insisted that the men responsible should be court-martialled. They were given a short term of imprisonment for manslaughter. Himmler subsequently quashed the sentence.

However, despite the lack of trust between the *Wehrmacht* and the SS, the army generals had to admit that during the early years of the war the SS were exceptional in bravery, discipline and soldierly bearing.

The first division entirely composed of SS was formed in October 1939. It was known as the SS-VT Division (motorised) and was commanded by General Paul Hausser. He was an 'old soldier' who had left the army in February 1932. Like many former army officers, he was a member of the 'Association of the Steel Helmet,' which

General (Obergruppenführer) Paul Hausser.

in 1934 became part of the reserve force of the SA. In 1934 Himmler, who was reorganising the SS, asked Hausser to organise an SS officers' school. His success in this resulted in his promotion to Inspector-General of the SS, an office he was holding when the war started.He was credited with being the founder of the *Waffen* (fighting) SS and was venerated as such.

The SS Division took part in the drive towards Rotterdam in May, 1940. They became part of the army's 9th Panzer Division while intercepting a French force in the south-west. The French were joined by retreating Dutch troops and the SS had the job of mopping up the last pockets of Franco-Dutch resistance. The division was then transferred to France where they breached a canal line defended by the British. They were accused of the assassination of British prisoners during the drive towards Dunkirk.

Subsequently attached to *Panzergruppe Kleist*, the SS took part in the advance on Paris. Eventually the motorised section travelled as far as the Spanish border. In December 1940, part of the division, the *Germania* Regiment and the SS Artillery Regiment joined the *Nordland* Regiment to form a new SS division named *Germania*. The original division was compensated for the loss of the regiment by the addition of the *Totenkopf* (Death's Head) Regiment. The division now became known as SS-Division *Deutschland*. But it was soon realised that there was a regiment with the same title and the name was changed to SS Division *Reich* in January 1941.

In March 1941, the division was stationed near Versoul in southern France but was soon moved to south-west Rumania. The motorised section travelled through Vienna and Budapest as far as the Jugoslav frontier where the rest of the division joined them. It had then become part of the 61st *Panzer Korps* which raced to Belgrade. The city surrendered to an assault group of the *Das Reich*, led by Captain Klingenberg, who was awarded the Knight's Cross. The division was then transferred to Poland where it became part of the huge force attacking Russia. It distinguished itself at the battle of Yalna, east of Smolensk, and subsequently took part in the bid to reach

Captain (Hauptsturmführer) Klingenberg

Moscow. The Russian winter stopped them within a short distance of the capital. Casualties were heavy, over 10,000 men being killed by Russian weaponry and the bitter weather.

In March 1942, the *Reich* Division was sent to north-west France to be transformed into a panzer-grenadier division. However, two battalions and an artillery group remained on the eastern front, where they fought until June 1942 when they joined the rest of the division, now known as SS-Panzer-Grenadier Division *Das Reich*.

Early in 1943, *Das Reich* joined the *Adolf Hitler* and *Totenkopf* divisions to become the 1st *Panzer Korps* which returned to the battle in the east. Russian armies were threatening the German forces in the Donetz Basin. Field-Marshal von Manstein, commander of the Army Group South, launched an attack with the 1st SS *Panzer Korps* at the head. It resulted in a Russian retreat and the recapture of Kharkov. *Das Reich* spearheaded an offensive near Orel and Kursk, but the Russian defence held.

Field-Marshal von Manstein

The division received a special commendation from von Manstein. Hitler told a group of dinner guests, 'I am proud when an army commander tells me his force is based on the SS *Das Reich* Division.'

In December 1943, the advance group of the *Das Reich* moved to Stablack in East Prussia where they made up for some of their huge losses. Apart from men, the division had lost an enormous amount of material. One notable feature was that many of the officers who had been with the division almost since its foundation had survived the war on the Russian front and were continuing to fight there under the name *Kämpfgruppe Reich*, also known as *Kämpfgruppe Lammerding*, their commander being General H B Lammerding, a friend of Himmler. Lammerding, the General nominally responsible for the Oradour massacre, was born in 1905 in Dortmund. he

90

trained as a civil engineer and joined the SA in 1931. For a while he was concerned with municipal construction at Leisnig in Saxony, but from 1931 he was entirely employed on Nazi concerns. In 1935 he left the SA and signed a contract with the SS to whom he was committed to serve until the age of 45. His subsequent career included instruction at the SS cadets' school at Brunswick. It was in October 1939 when Lammerding attracted the attention of General Hausser and was given command of a battalion of pioneers of the SS *Totenkopf* Division which took part in the war in France. His services were recognised by the award of the Iron

General *(Obergruppenführer)* H B Lammerding

Cross 1st Class. In August 1942 as colonel he took over command of the SS *Thule* Regiment of infantry and after several engagements in the Kharkov region he was awarded the *'Deutsche Kreuz.'*

In July 1943, Himmler created some special 'anti-terrorist' units to combat partisan activity in Russia. In charge of these units was SS Police-General von dem Bach-Zalewski. Lammerding was his chief of staff. Their activities involved ruthless slaughter and destruction. One of the last orders given by Lammerding to the SS Brigade *Langemark* before he left read:

'The inhabitants of Mitkowsky and Klembowka are to be removed from their homes and all resistance will be repressed. All the dwellings in those areas will be burned and the remains razed by tanks.'

In other words, he expected the villages to be erased from the map, like Lidice, and no mercy should be shown to anyone who resisted.

***(Obergruppenführer)* Police-General von dem Bach-Zalewski.**

Civilians being rounded up by the SS.

In December 1943, the *Das Reich* Division in France had over 20,000 men and 200 tanks. Their ranks included many men from Alsace-Lorraine who had been conscripted with other men from occupied countries. (Alsace-Lorraine was still regarded as part of Germany at that time.) The Alsatians had been called up in various age groups since 1942 to serve in the German forces. The Vichy government protested several times about the recruitment of Frenchmen but there was no reply from Germany. The fact that these protests received no publicity led the people of Alsace-Lorraine to believe they had been totally abandoned by France. Some of the conscripts managed to get away to Switzerland and unoccupied France. If they were captured they were shot. In October 1943, the Germans decided to confiscate all the possessions of the deserters and their families were sent to Poland. This almost stopped the desertions. Yet a few of the young Alsatians were helped by the Resistance to escape from the *Das Reich* training camp at Bordeaux.

In January 1944, a large number of 18 years old Alsatians were sent to SS training camps to make up for the losses in

Russia. Some went to the *Das Reich* camp at Stablack and others were trained elsewhere. Most of them eventually joined the division at Bordeaux. The trainloads of recruits, many still in civilian clothes, were transported in cattle trucks.

The training was rapid and incomplete. It was considered that the newcomers would complete their training when the division was in action. Then they would soon learn how the strictly-disciplined SS carried out brutal activities without question. However, despite the influx of new recruits, the *Das Reich* division was dispirited. The hard core were battle weary and depressed by the loss of comrades in Russia and families who were killed by the bombing of German towns and cities. The efforts to make good SS men from reluctant recruits imposed a burden on the officers and NCOs.

In the Spring of 1944, the Germans were aware that an invasion of France was imminent. Apart from aerial reconnassance revealing a massing of men and war material in the south of England and reports from agents in Britain and the USA, documents taken from captured maquisards proved that the great battle was near. It was assumed that suitable weather conditions for the attack would be between 1 May and 30 June.

General Blaskowitz.

Hitler was convinced that the main onslaught would be in the region of Calais. However, the German forces were spread over a wide area north of the Loire, under the command of Rommel. They were known as Army Group B. The forces south of the Loire, Army Group G under General Blaskowitz, were comparatively light, comprising thirteen infantry divisions, of which five were in training, one light motorised SS division and three SS armoured divisions, of which *Das Reich* was one.

The 11th Armoured Division was based near Bordeaux and the 9th near Avignon. The *Das Reich* installed their headquarters at Montauban and were expected to be in a position to support the others if needed. Apart from a possible

Mediterranean landing, there was a growing threat from the Resistance. The Gestapo were well aware that the maquis would exert their full force as soon as the invasion started, trying to cut communications between one army group and another.

In May 1944 *Das Reich* comprised three panzer-grenadier regiments with battalions of tanks, artillery (including mobile guns, flat-topped and difficult to hit), motorised reconnaissance and signals, together with catering, repairs, medical and sanitation units.

Field-Marshal Sperrle

Field-Marshal Sperrle had ordered an utterly ruthless treatment of civilians, involved or sympathising with the 'terrorists', including the burning of their homes. Lammerding's orders were to keep the lines of communication open at any price. In the event of a landing he would move his division as rapidly as possible to the front concerned, spreading wide to deal with all possible resistance.

SS officers swearing the oath of allegiance to Adolf Hitler. Men living up to their oath were prepared to implement the most outrageous orders.

CHAPTER FIVE

Atrocities

On 2 May Lammerding received a coveted decoration, the *Ritterkreuz* or Knight's Cross for having, on the Russian front, ' led a detachment of the *Das Reich* Division in a rapid movement to stop the Russians breaking through at Jampol.' There was a celebration in the officers' mess at Montauban with copious champagne and the singing of SS songs. That same day, a series of atrocities in the south west was attributed to the *Das Reich* Division.

Before the division's arrival in the south, the *Brehmer* Division and the 76th Brigade known as the *Jesser* (the names were of the commanding officers) had been in action against the Resistance. But their components were weak, each comprising one or two SS police regiments, which included Russians who had been given the choice of fighting with the Germans or going to a concentration camp. Their efforts were insignificant compared with those of the *Das Reich* Division.

The crimes committed by *Das Reich* usually followed a scenario. the men involved had been specially trained for ruthless acts of vengeance against civilians wherever they were suspected of aiding or sympathising with the 'terrorists.' It is possible, however, that some of the atrocities attributed to *Das Reich* were committed by units of the *Wehrmacht*, who could be equally ruthless.

The usual *Das Reich* practice was:

(1)	To surround a chosen village.

(2)	To occupy the principal offices, – the *mairie*, the police station, etc.

(3)	To assemble the population, together with people living in the neighbourhood, using the town crier to announce the order.

Then came the killing, looting and burning. In one case they shut the women and children in the church but they were later released. It is certain that Lammerding was aware of and approved these measures. On 2 May a detachment of the 1st Battalion of the 2nd Regiment stationed at Caussade entered the village of Montpezat-de-Quercy. The battalion commander,

Major Tetsch, led a number of tanks and other tracked vehicles through the village under the nervous gaze of the people. It was not the first time the SS had come their way but it soon became apparent that this was a different, more menacing visit.

The convoy stopped outside the *mairie* and the mayor was seized and marched away. Meanwhile the convoy divided into groups which called at farms in the neighbourhood. With loud cries the SS forced the inhabitants to leave the buildings to which they set fire. In all, about a dozen farms around the village were destroyed. The village people were assembled in the main square before soldiers armed with machine-guns and rifles. The SS looted and burnt a number of large houses. At one house they killed M Bonnet, an elderly man, and his granddaughter, aged 2, and threw their bodies into the fire. The presbytery, which contained valuable antiques and books, was destroyed and the parish priest Father Schap,was arrested. He was made to stand facing a wall with his hands up while an NCO poked the muzzle of a machine-gun into his back. An officer ordered him to reveal where arms were hidden in the village. The priest protested that there was no arms cache that he knew of and he was released, terrified.

When the SS eventually left the village they took twenty-two men with them. They were brutally beaten and deported. Four people had been killed. It was not until some time later that the villagers learnt that there had been a skirmish between the SS and some maquisards about two kilometres away, which may have been the reason for the raid.

From the middle of May, the Gestapo at Montauban and its detachment at Cahors gathered information about the Resistance in the Department of Lot. They had the assistance of fifteen Frenchmen, of whom one had spent several weeks with the maquis in the Cabrerets region. At the beginning of May, Lieutenant Muller of the Gestapo believed he had sufficient information for a drive against the Maquis in Lot, with the help of the *Das Reich* Division. Eight places were pinpointed for action. They included the villages of Blars, Cabrerets, Lauzés, Terrou, Latronquière and Gramat where, it was reported, there was a large number of maquis with caches of arms, vehicles and even an American tanker with 18,000 litres of fuel. In fact, it was alleged that the 'terrorists' controlled the region under a helpless *gendarmerie*. It was believed that the villagers

German firing squad in operation in Poland.

supported the 'terrorists' and if this were true all the men would be rounded up and sent to a concentration camp.

This large-scale operation, involving the Gestapo and the SS, was launched on the evening of 10 May. During the night a detachment moving from Caussade was joined by men of the headquarters of the division at Montauban. Another group, composed of members of the 1st Battalion of the *Der Führer* Regiment, had Adolf Diekmann as the commander. They had been stationed at Valence d'Agen. They were joined by other groups from the regiment and the two columns converged at the village of Le Bourg, north of Figéac. Between 4 and 7 a.m., the SS descended on the suspect villages where they searched in vain for the nests of maquis and caches of arms and vehicles.

At Cabrerets, at about 4 a.m., the detachment of the 1st Battalion killed a Spanish farmhand and arrested the farmer and his domestic on the grounds that they had cared for wounded maquisards. They looted several farms and burnt one, for no apparent reason.

Lauzès was surrounded, the police were disarmed and the phone lines cut. All the men were assembled in the square while houses were looted. There was some random shooting and two women were killed during a tour of nearby farms. They were Mme Moncontré, aged 50, and her daughter Berthe (20) who were tending their sheep. A bit farther on, M Lalo (66) was shot while working in his garden. No word was spoken before the soldiers fired. Then, to their enormous relief, the men who had been lined up in the square were allowed to go after a brief examination of their papers.

The procedure was the same at Orneac. The men were assembled while houses were ransacked. The men were released, apart from the mayor and two others who were taken away.

At Blars it was a different story, after the village had been looted the SS took twenty-one people away with them.

Cardillac was visited twice. The SS rounded up the men at 7 a.m. Two young men who tried to run away were shot, women working in the fields were fired on, one being killed and another badly wounded. The next day another troop arrived and the men were again rounded up.

At Sagnac an SS officer ordered the mayor to produce a list of Jews and strangers in the town. There were none. However, all the men, except those over 60, were assembled. The SS took away about eighty of them, of whom half were later released while the rest were deported. There was random shooting in the village and two women were killed.

After the customary round-up at Saint-Céré, some men were beaten. Twenty-four inhabitants, including four women, were arrested and deported.

The worst incidents occurred on 12 May in the hamlet of Niel. The SS burst into the house of M and Mme Gratacap. They were at table with their five children. Without a word of explanation, they took the parents into a neighbouring wood and shot them.

At Garrigue the Carrayou family, with their three children, were working in a field near their home when the SS arrived. Without any apparent motive, they killed them all. Two other people in the same hamlet were shot.

The SS arrived at Saint-Félix in the afternoon. They ransacked several houses in the fading hope of' finding the elusive arms cache. M Rives (53) was shot and they took eight people to Figéac where they shut them in a cave for the night. Their guards fired into the obscurity from time to time and the prisoners had to back into crevices to avoid being hit. However, one of them, a M Barrie, was killed. The next day two of the older people were released and the other five deported. They never returned.

At Latronquière the toll was one killed and eighty deported. The hamlet of Groscassan was completely destroyed by fire. Death and destruction were suffered by other hamlets and some cases of rape were reported. All the people taken during this operation were removed to Figéac and then to Montauban where they were put in some barracks which had been converted into a prison. They were people of various ages, including priests, policemen and two women. During their imprisonment two young men were removed and shot and others were tortured. Eventually, for no apparent reason, the SS released several dozen prisoners and deported the rest. The massive operation to 'purge' the Lot of its maquis with their weapons ended with none of the objectives achieved.

The random shooting in the exercise was probably carried

Funeral of *Das Reich* soldiers killed in operations against the maquis at Guéret, June 1944.

out by young soldiers, often uneducated and only partly trained, who were given sophisticated weapons to 'play with' and may have been excited by what they could do by simply squeezing a trigger. If they killed in error a reprimand was highly unlikely and they soon became immune to the sight of bleeding corpses for whom they had been responsible. If there was no actual motive for the killings they could invent one, such as 'they supported the terrorists' but it is unlikely that they were ever called upon to account for their random killings. It has also to be remembered that fear was involved. They were not only afraid of displaying anything but strict obedience to order, but although the superiority of the SS was evident they suffered casualties by snipers and ambushes in May 1944. In fact, about twenty men died at the hands of the 'terrorists' and there was considerable loss of vehicles and other material.

Shortly afterwards, the Gestapo were informed that various units of resistance were to be found in the Dordogne and Lot-et-Garonne. The *Das Reich* Division was again called upon to help. The 1st Battalion of the *Der Führer* Regiment was nominated for the job by the regimental commander. On 21 May, four companies of the battalion under Captains Kahn, Scholtz, Schwartz and Rosenstock, moved to Fumel in the north, accompanied by the Gestapo. The four companies divided, each covering a different area. Diekmann with other officers of the battalion and the Gestapo, set up their headquarters in a hotel near the village of Gavaudun. They kept in radio contact with the company commanders. This time they were lucky. A small arms cache was found in the house of M Abouty at Devillac. He was stripped and hung by his feet while the SS beat him until he was unconscious. Then he was loaded into a truck bound for Cahors. It is assumed that he died on the way and was dumped because he never arrived.

There were particularly brutal scenes at Fontenelles. The SS arrived au 4 a.m. and broke open a recently built vault in the cemetery, searching for arms. It was empty so they ransacked the church, breaking down the door. Then followed the usual looting. Bicycles, radios, food and linen were among the things loaded into trucks. The soldiers stole all the jewellery they could lay their hands on. As no arms cache was found, the mayor was arrested and all the people were assembled in the village square. Meanwhile the surrounding countryside was scoured and a

Captain (Hauptsturmführer) **Kahn (centre) was engaged in committing atrocities against French civilians prior to Oradour. In the front, nursing what appears to be a cat, is Lieutenant** *(Untersturmführer)* **Heinz Barth who played a major part in carrying out reprisals.**

patrol found two FFI men and a parachuted Canadian NCO in a wood.

The captors returned to Fontenelles in triumph with their captives and the three men were brought before Captain Kahn, the commander of the third company. After questioning, the Canadian was separated from the other two who were thrown about, kicked and beaten with cries of 'terrorists!' Eventually the battered, bleeding men were taken to a house where ropes had been fixed to beams in the ceiling. The luckless FFI men were suspended by their feet, beaten and allowed to fall on their heads. At mid-day, the men, barely able to walk, almost dragged by their tormentors, were put against a wall with other men, while a squad stood before them, fingering their weapons. Then, as if rehearsed, the church clock started to strike and through the broken door of the church came the sound of organ music played by an SS man. At the same time, a gramophone stolen from a teacher was brought to the square and a record of the *Marseillaise* was played. The firing squad continued to finger their weapons before the terrified men at the wall. Other SS men consumed stolen food and wine.

There was another sorting out of the people in the square. Men under 16 and over 60 were released, together with the women. Eventually, to their immense relief, the others were told they could go – that is, all except the two maquisards, the Canadian and two brothers, Jean and Maurice Scholtz.

Leaving Fontenelles at about 4 p.m., the SS moved to the east, regrouping around Frayssinat-le-Gélat, a village of about 400 inhabitants. The men were assembled in the square on the orders of Captain Kahn. As usual, there was looting while latecomers were battered with rifle butts. Identity papers were being examined when a shot was fired from a window and a soldier was wounded. Kahn immediately lined up his men with their machine-guns while several of them rushed into the house from which the shot had been fired. They found three women, of whom one, Mme Agathe Pailles, was 80 years old. It seemed that the old woman, scared by the behaviour of the SS, had fired a shotgun at them. The house was set on fire while ropes were fixed to telephone poles near the church. Women and children were brought into the square to witness the hanging of the old woman and her two nieces, whose bodies were flung into their blazing home. Then, for no apparent reason, Mme Yvonne Vidilles was seized by her hair, dragged along the ground and shot with a revolver.

Kahn selected ten men to be lined up against a wall. An interpreter announced that the men were to be executed. The youngest was a youth of 15, Guy Mourgues, whose father begged Kahn to let him embrace him for the last time. Kahn agreed with a grin and the two men were shot with the others. The dead were stripped of their money, watches and rings. A pit was dug for the bodies, the grandfather of the Mourgues youth

SS troops arriving in a French village.

being ordered to help fill it in.

The campaign of shooting and destruction of property occupied the majority of the regiments until the end of May. This exasperated the divisional staff who felt that the training progamme should have been completed. Protests were made to Army Group G about the use of frontline soldiers against civilians. Shortage of fuel was also holding up the training. The isolated excursions revealed a lack of co-ordination between the various units and it seemed unlikely that *Das Reich* could move as a well-organised division when they were called into action.

There was also a shortage or vital transport, particularly of trucks and tractors for the guns. In mid-May the division received thirty-seven Panzer Vs and fifty-five Panzer IVs. The force was also strengthened by thirty *Stürmgeschützen* –

SS troops begin a search of the houses looking for arms.

turretless tanks, low on the ground and so difficult to disable with anti-tank weapons.

At the beginning of 1944 there were 1,480 prisoners in 'the best-guarded prison in France', the prison of Eysses, near Villeneuve-sur-Lot. They were all resistants who had been sentenced by French courts. In February there was a big escape bid at the jail. It failed, Darnand, the head of the militia and Secretary-General of the Départment for the maintenance of order under the Vichy government, visited Eysses and saw the prisoners in their cells. He was assured there would be no reprisals but twelve were taken out and shot when he left. Vichy was afraid that another escape bid might succeed, with the prisoners joining the Resistance, so it was decided to hand them over to the Germans.

On 18 May, thirty-six prisoners regarded as hostages were transported to Blois and handed over to the 1st Battalion of the *Der Führer* Regiment, under Diekmann. They took the prisoners to the railway station at Penne-d'Agenais, a distance of about seven kilometres. Although most of the men were conveyed in trucks, the party, including a number of sick and elderly men, were marched there and beaten en route to keep up the pace.

One of the sick, a M. Huergas, fainted and was despatched with a bullet in the back of his neck. This was only a sample of what the prisoners of Eysses were to suffer during their deportation. Many died in the concentration camp to which they were sent.

As D-Day approached, Allied bombers attacked the rail network, assisted by sabotaging maquisards. On 1 June maquisards of the Lot attacked the railway centre at Capdenac.

A detachment of the 2nd Battalion of the 2nd Panzer Regiment patrolled the roads of the Lot. Towards 4 p.m, the SS entered the village of Limogne. It was market day and many people had come in from the surrounding hamlets. There was immediate panic, the brutality of the SS being widely known. Most of the men tried to run away. The soldiers jumped out of the trucks and opened fire and six men were killed. They included Charles Vernhat (17) and Lambert Puel (14). The SS did not linger in the village, to the immense relief of the community. They moved north in the direction of Figéac. During their passage through various villages they fired haphazardly, killing one person at Cardrieu and two at Frontenac. They spent the night at Figéac. The next day they combed the region north of Figéac. At about 6.30 a.m. the tail end of the column was attacked by members of the FFI. A truck was damaged but there were no casualties. The SS immediately set out to pursue the attackers. There were about twenty of them and they quickly disappeared into a wood. The soldiers failed to find any of them. In the afternoon the village of Cambyrat was looted and twenty-nine farms and houses were burnt.

At Saint-Bressou the men were grouped in the square and papers were examined. Houses were looted and set on fire. One man was shot in the street. The SS fired random bursts of machine-gun fire in the surrounding fields and woods and continued northwards. The village of Terrou was almost completely destroyed by fire. The next day, 3 June, two vehicles left Figéac early in the morning, heading for Aurillac. They were carrying eight SS and a woman. She was the wife of Lieutenant Hohne, commander of the lst Company of the SS Pioneer

Battalion. For some strange reason he wanted her to be close to him and thought she might enjoy the trip. It was a tragic mistake.

Shortly after leaving Figéac the two vehicles arrived at the bridge of Colombiers. The road then went through a valley which the FFI had used for ambushes and a group of them opened fire on the vehicles. Seven of the nine occupants were killed, including Hohne and his wife. The two who escaped, managed to get back to Figéac to report the incident. A reprisal exercise was immediately organised. Less than an hour later a column of thirty armoured vehicles and a motor-cycle platoon set out for the location of the killings. At the nearest house they flung open the door and tossed a grenade among the inhabitants. A bit farther on two old people, M and Mme Gibrat were shot in their chairs and their farm destroyed.

Arriving at Viazac, the SS fired at the doors and windows. Six men and a woman were taken to the scene of the ambush and shot. The convoy arrived at the hamlet of Cayla at about 11 a.m., firing at both sides of the street. The Lacombe farm was burnt and the farmer killed. His wife and children were wounded. Another farmer, M. Truel, was also shot and his wife and two sons, who had been wounded, were flung into the blazing farm house. The young people of the hamlet fled into the woods, leaving behind two old folk, M Rives and Mme Ganil, who were shot. The Abbé Lacarinière was also shot, together with anyone the convoy happened to pass on the road. Seven men, of between the ages of 20 and 56, were shot in this manner, innocent of what was happening. The village of Bagnac was sprayed with bullets. A workman on the roadside was killed, so, too, was M Heliés, a grower, who was working on his land.

Further killings, lootings and burnings followed without any apparent attempt to find the men responsible for the ambush. None of the victims were questioned before they were shot. In fact, it was not a military exercise but more an operation to terrorize the people in the locality.

CHAPTER SIX

Resistance

On D-Day, 6 June, no direct orders from Army Group G were received by *Das Reich* immediately. There was exaltation in the streets of Montauban, where most of the regiments had grouped and the officers soon became aware of the landings in the north. There was a feeling of relief that the final battle had started, but there was concern over the lack of transport for the drive, as well as inadequate equipment and incomplete training of the newcomers to the division. Civilian trucks and cars were requisitioned. One tank company was in Germany collecting Panzer Vs.

The division waited through the day while reports were received of the rising of the Resistance in southern and central France. The Division was eventually ordered to move towards the Normandy battlefield, crushing all resistance en route. Their task included the securing of communications between the units stationed between the Atlantic and the Mediterranean.

Panther tanks of the *Das Reich* at Montauban prior to the drive to Normandy.

The direct route to the battlefield covered 450 miles, and the division had to cross a vast region renowned for the strength of the maquis who were dedicated to block every troop movement. The Resistance had sprung into action on 6 June as a result of coded messages broadcast from London.

Their strategy was based on two plans – the *Plan Vert* (green plan) and the *Bibendum Plan*. The *Plan Vert* aimed at paralysing the railways. On the morning of 6 June the Paris – Toulouse line

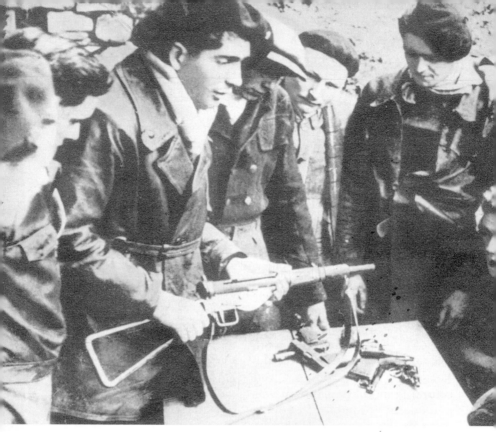

Resistance members undergoing training in small arms at a hidden location.

was cut in several places, as also were the connections between Limoges and Chatroux, Brive and Montauban. The Clairmont Ferrand – Brive line had been severed in May and the Limoges – Angoulême and Limoges – Poitiers lines were cut on 8 June.

It was hoped that this action would effectively delay the transport of tanks and other material destined for the Normandy front. However, the Germans became proficient at repairing with the minimum of delay. The Resistance made the mistake of spacing the cuts too far apart and the trains managed to gather some speed between them.

The *Bibendum Plan* aimed at paralysing road transport and was effective for six weeks after D-Day. The Allies hoped the FFI could bring about a delay of 48 hours in the arrival of enemy reinforcements. In fact, the average delay was five or six days and reached ten days for some SS units. The Germans, seeking a passage through the blockades were often obliged to split into small groups who arrived in Normandy in complete disarray. The 2nd Panzer Artillery Regiment took to the road on 7 June. The 1st and 3rd battalions of the *Der Führer* Regiment and the 1st Battalion of the *Deutschland* Regiment started on 8 June. The tanks of the 2nd Panzer Regiment left Caussade on the same day.

When the regiments of the *Das Reich* division took to the road, the maquis clashed with them continuously. In spite of the big difference in means and numbers, the FFI had the advantage of their knowledge of the territory. They managed to inflict considerable damage on the SS, slowing them down on the sinuous roads of the Dordogne where many ambushes were laid.

The SS executed all the maquisards they captured, sometimes after torturing them. The Resistance could not halt the movement of the *Das Reich* to the north, although the division beat all records for tardiness in arriving at the Normandy battlefield. On 7 June the advance guard of *Das Reich* clashed

Captured Maquisards await execution.

A Resistance camp hidden away in the woods. Above: cleaning a variety of weapons; below: a suspected colaborater is being tried before a 'court'.

with the 1st company of the 1st Battalion of the FFI of Basse-Corrèze near the Souillac bridge. The previous day the FFI had inflicted heavy losses of men and material on a German detachment at the same spot. The SS columns marching on both flanks of the main convoy met with the same difficulties. The one in the east arrived at the bridge at 6.30 a.m. and encountered the 3rd company of the resistants of Basse-Corrèze led by Lieutenant Destre. The SS had to wait for the arrival of several tanks and were held up for four hours.

In the west, a company of 80 vehicles, preceded by *schützpanzerwagen* (small armoured cars) was held up at the Groslejac bridge and lost one vehicle and six men. Near Rouffignac the maquis company 'Bernard' destroyed a truck, and two mobile machine-guns. They killed some SS and wounded others.

Surprised and furious at these attacks, the SS fired at every living thing. Their victims were people of all ages and many homes were destroyed. On 8 June a detachment of six armoured vehicles arrive at the hamlet of Donadieu in the commune of Gramat. The people fled as soon as they heard the sound of approaching tanks and took shelter in the woods. A man of sixty-five stayed on his farm and was shot. The SS burnt nearly all the farms in the locality together with barns and stables containing livestock.

The farm of Gabaudet, about 500 metres from Donadieu was an assembly point of local resistants. It is not known how the SS found out about it. They may have been told by a local informer, or it may have been sheer chance. The farm was quickly surrounded and ninety-one maquisards were captured. After questionings and beatings, eleven were shot, the rest were taken first to Tulle and later towards Limoges. Many of the captives were policemen or airmen. To their utter surprise and relief, nearly all of them were released before the convoy reached Limoges. The remainder were deported. This was an example of the increasingly indecisive attitude of the SS officers.

During the afternoon of 8 June an SS convoy captured five maquisards in a car. One of them, a youth of twenty, managed to get away but the others were killed. A short while later the convoy came upon a certain Doctor Aicenbaum, a Jewish partisan refugee who had been attending wounded maquisards. He was shot on the spot, as were some other Jews who had

Jacques Chapou.

come south, feeling they were in safer territory.

The SS were held up for a long time just outside the town of Calviac. They took their revenge at the nearby hamlet of Rouffillac. At the Hôtel Marty six women and five little girls were sheltering terrified by the sound of fighting. The SS brought them out into the street. Mme Yvonne Marty protested and they were all pushed into a café and shot, after which they were drenched with petrol and set alight. Some were only wounded and screamed. Two little girls, badly burnt, were recovered and taken to the Sarlat hospital where one, Irene Poukchliakoff aged seven, miraculously survived.

Many other people were killed in their homes and all the houses were burnt.

At this time most of the maquisards were members of the *FTPF (Francs Tireurs et Partisans Francais)* and were mostly Communists. In the Spring of 1944 it was estimated that there were about five thousand of them in the Corrèze. There were many former army officers and NCOs in the region and an officer from London did his best to persuade them to join the FTPF so that they could be led by experienced men. But it was of no avail, probably because of the politics of the maquisards. So civil servants, simple workmen and even peasants improvised as officers in the FTPF of the Corrèze.

Some smaller cadres were formed. The army officers created the *ORA (Organisation de Résistance de l'Armée)*, while professors and teachers had their own maquis.The winter of 1943-44 had been very cold and hard for the maquis. The Germans made many arrests, executions and deportations.

In the Lot the principal resistance movement carried the title 'Libération', with Jacques Chapou, also known as 'Philippe' as its leader. At the beginning of 1944 he took command of a number of maquis, grouped under the title *Mouvements Unis de Resistance*. In March he decided to mount a military operation.

CHAPTER SEVEN

A Fatal Encounter

After a successful attack on Carjac, a town of about a thousand people, Maquis leader Jean-Jacques Chapou decided to try a bigger target. He decided on the town of Tulle situated in the River Corrèze valley. The first objective was a barracks occupied by militiamen who soon surrendered and were allowed to leave, heading for Limoges.

The second assault was on a school occupied by German soldiers. The FTP fired incendiary shells andthe school was soon ablaze. About forty soldiers came out to surrender. At about the same time soldiers higher up the street opened fire and the men who had surrendered were mown down, suffering multiple injuries. The *Das Reich* Division, received a report of the battle and on 9 June sent the 2nd Motorised Reconnaissance Battalion, the HQ company of the 1st battalion of the 2nd Panzer Regiment and two batteries of the 2nd *Panzerartillery* Regiment.

The maquisards were overpowered and, as the SS claimed that the soldiers who had been at the school were deliberately mutilated, General Lammerding ordered the execution of 120 men by hanging. Ropes with nooses were slung from lamp

Tulle road bridge where the hangings took place. The SS took photographs and this drawing was made from one of them.

posts in the street.

About 400 men were rounded up and 120 were selected by the Gestapo. The hangings were stopped at 99 because no more suitable ropes could be found. The men who were spared thought they might be released but were taken to Limoges and later to Poitiers. Their eventual destination was Compiègne where they were packed into trucks with 2,500 other deportees and taken to Dachau concentration camp. A hundred and one of them died, either on the train or at the camp.

The situation in Limoges was tense. The city's rail centre had

Major (Sturmbahnführer) Helmut Kämpfe. His capture by the Resistance was to spark the atrocity at Oradour.

been hit by saboteurs and there had been several attacks on German vehicles, many of the occupants being killed.

The *Der Führer* Regiment, under Colonel Stadler, arrived in the city early on the morning of 9 June. Stadler set up his headquarters at the Hôtel Central. Later in the day, he ordered the 3rd Battalion, under Major Helmut Kämpfe, to go to the town of Guéret in the north-east, where there had been a battle between the army and the resistants.

The maquisards had launched their first attack on the German garrison at Guéret on 7 June. It was an easier campaign than that at Tulle because no militiamen were involved. In fact, the attackers were helped by students of a police college who moved *en masse* to join them. The Germans had been overcome within a few hours and the maquisards took control of the town.

The *Wehrmacht* launched an attack to retake the town on the morning of 8 June. Sections of the 121st Infantry Division were involved, together with the *Jesser* Brigade, but they were repulsed, despite a bombardment of the town by the Luftwaffe. There was another bombing on 9 June and the planes flew low, machine-gunning the streets. The soldiers attacked again and managed to get into the centre of the town, rounding up the resistants.

On the way to Guéret, Kämpfe's men encountered four trucks carrying twenty-nine young maquisards. Only two of them were armed but the SS shot them all at the roadside. They met two more trucks, driven by maquisards who fled after firing several bursts which wounded an officer. The abandoned trucks contained captured German soldiers and officials and some collaborators. Two of them were dead and others wounded. Doctor Muller, an SS doctor, was ordered to take a vehicle and return to Limoges with the wounded. When the SS entered Guéret they found their services were no longer needed, the town being in the hands of the Germans again. They could only turn round and go back.

Kämpfe, who had been driving a stolen Talbot car, decided to return to Limoges as quickly as possible. He overtook Doctor Muller's vehicle and was some way ahead when, near the hamlet of La Bussière, about fifteen miles from Limoges, he met a vehicle coming the other way. He was immediately surrounded by a number of armed maquisards, led by Sergeant Jean Canou, a miner. They had been blowing up a bridge at Brignac.

This was Canou's description of what happened:

'It was almost dark when we saw a car approaching. Our driver pulled up and we all jumped out as the car stopped. To our surprise, the driver of the car was a German officer. He made no attempt to resist . We put him in our truck and soon left the main road to take the road to Cheissoux.

'The German was a tall, handsome type who smiled when we bundled him into our truck and carried on. Just after we left the main road we heard heavy vehicles passing.'

Canou's camp was at Cheissoux and he handed over the captive to his chiefs there. He never saw him again.

Kämpfe probably smiled because he thought his captors would soon come face to face with his men. He had not counted on the truck leaving the main road. His careless behaviour was quite out of key with his otherwise intelligent and successful military career. If he had not been so foolish as to drive alone in country well-known for its maquis activity, Oradour might have been spared.

Helmut Kämpfe was born in 1909 and started his working, life as a printer – later the owner of a printing works. He joined

Major (Sturmbahnführer) **Helmut Kämpfe. He was popular among his fellow officers and men.**

the Nazi party early in his career. He was tall, strong and handsome and, being fascinated by soldiering and weapons, he joined an infantry regiment in 1934. In May 1939 he joined the SS as a member of the 7th Regiment of Reconnaissance. He was promoted a sub-lieutenant in 1940 and lieutenant a year later. In June 1941 he was on the staff of the reconnaissance section of the *Das Reich* Division and took part in the attempt to reach Moscow. He was promoted captain in April 1942 and in 1943 took part in the great tank battle at Kursk. His conduct in the Russian campaign resulted in his being promoted major in September 1943. His awards included the *Ritterkreuz* and the Iron Cross 1st and 2nd class.

So this formidable soldier, who foolishly drove his car unaccompanied and was captured by a party of civilians, was a hero not only of the *Das Reich* Division but also of the SS as a whole. His loss was a shattering blow.

Doctor Muller was the first to came across Kämpfe's empty car with its engine still running. It had been abandoned by the maquisards because only one of them could drive. A Schmeisser machine-gun with an empty magazine was on a seat. There was no blood or other signs of a struggle. When the convoy arrived it was felt that Kämpfe must be somewhere near and the neighbourhood was scoured. Doctor Muller reported Kämpfe's loss to Colonel Stadler when he arrived in Limoges. Kämpfe had been Stadler's adjutant in Russia and he decided that a thorough search must be made. He sent members of the local militia, who knew the territory, to join in the search. This went on through the night, tracked vehicles being used and flares fired. The people living in the area were terrified as the searchers burst open doors and fetched them out.

The road down which Kämpfe was driven immediately following his capture, thus ensuring his complete disappearance.

The farm of Pierre Malaguise, near the hamlet of La Bussière, was invaded and, because the soldiers thought he gave unsatisfactory answers to their questions, he was taken outside and shot by the roadside. A similar fate was suffered by Pierre Just, another farmer. Both men were married and each had five children.

The search was in vain and the men involved eventually had to return to Limoges, where confusion and fury reigned over Kämpfe's loss. Stadler ordered Major Weidinger to return to Tulle where Lammerding was spending the night. After a nervous journey in the dark, in a field car with a motor-cycle escort, Weidinger reported Kämpfe's loss to Lammerding who ordered an immediate resumption of the search.

What actually happened to Kämpfe is unknown. But it is certain that somewhere, somehow he was killed. It was rumoured that his captors locked him in a pig sty and he was still there on 28 June. He was said to have been shot by a sentry shortly afterwards when he tried to escape. But there has never been confirmation of this. The SS recorded that he was 'missing in action against terrorists.'

When Kämpfe's widow visited Cheissoux and other parts years later in an effort to find his grave, she came up against a wall of silence.

During the night of 7-8 June a group of maquisards had tried to blow up a viaduct carrying the Limoges-Angoulème railway line over the Vienne valley near Saint-Junien. The attempt failed, so they tried again early on the morning, of the eighth and managed to wreck the line, derailing a freight train. The engine fell into the river. Although trains could no longer cross, passengers could go over on foot to join a train at the other end. Among the first passengers to cross from a train from Angoulème to board one which would take them to Limoges were ten armed Germans. The maquisards, concealed in a small wood, opened fire on them. The other passengers scattered while shots were exchanged. Two of the Germans were killed and five ran back to the train they had left. The other three, carrying the bodies of their comrades, got on the waiting train and reached Limoges at about 10 p.m.

The next morning, 9 June, soldiers boarded an armoured train in Limoges and set out for Saint-Junien. They were accompanied by Lieutenant Wickers of the Gestapo and an interpreter named Hübsch. Mid-way, they stopped at a small station and Hübsch phoned the stationmaster at Saint-Junien, ordering him to summon the mayor and the police commissioner to be ready with a map of the town when the train arrived.

The saboteurs, who had taken over the *mairie* as a symbolic gesture of being in charge of the town, hurriedly left when they were told that an armoured train was coming. On arrival, the Germans were met by M Gibouin, who was deputising for the mayor, together with the police commissioner and the chief officer of the gendarmerie. They were frisked and locked in separate rooms at the station.

Wickers questioned Gibouin and the gendarmerie chief separately about the situation in the town, which had a population of about 20,000. Asked if there were 'terrorists' in the town, Gibouin is believed to have replied, 'There are at least 1,800 here.' This extraordinary statement, quite untrue, may have saved Saint-Junien from severe reprisals. The Germans did not want a battle at this stage. However, Wickers prepared for trouble. He ordered the rounding up of a hundred men to dig trenches. Fifty actually appeared, most of them elderly, and had to dig under guard until the early afternoon when they were discharged.

News had been received that the lst Battalion of the *Der Führer* Regiment, under Major Diekmann which had been travelling on the west of the main SS drive to the north, was on its way from Rochechouart. When they arrived, Diekmann discussed the situation with Wickers. He also interviewed some nervous local officials and decided to set up his headquarters at the Hôtel de la Gare. The SS filled up their vehicles and jerry cans with petrol at

Adolf Diekmann as a Captain (*Hauptsturmführer*). He was a close friend of Kämpfe.

the garages. They amused themselves and terrified the people by indulging in a grenade-throwing exercise in the town centre.

Early on the morning of the 10th, Diekmann was ordered to report to his regimental headquarters in Limoges. On arrival he joined in the general indignation over Kämpfe's loss and immediately associated it with what two men had told him in Saint-Junien. They said an important German officer was a prisoner of the maquis at Oradour and was to be publicly executed that day. The whole population of the village was involved and there were important 'terrorists' leaders among them.

The identity of the informers has never been established. Confirmation of their action was given in an American news sheet or magazine called *Siegrunen*. A photocopy of the article concerned was sent to me by the editor of an American magazine in which a review of my original book appeared. It had been sent to him with a letter from the author who described my book as 'the standard French-Jew diatribe on the subject'. He said he had got his information from German 'eye-witness' accounts and from the history of the *Der Führer* Regiment by Major Otto Weidinger. A few extracts from the book are worth quoting, although there are some obvious distortions of the facts:

> 'On the morning of 10 June two Frenchmen arrived at the command post of 1 Der Führer bringing information. The battalion C.O. Sturmbannführer *Adolph Diekmann, a very close friend of Stubaf. Kämpfe, interrogated them. They advised him that an important German officer was held by the Maquis in the town of Oradour and further, that the town was an armed communist camp with even the women toting guns and dressed in military jackets and steel helmets.*

A fantastic statement in the article was that a 'scouting party' had found a burnt-out building 'on the edge of' the town which had been a German dressing station. Inside were the bodies of German wounded and medics who had been shackled together and burned alive! There is not the slightest evidence to support this.

The article also stated that the church was packed with explosives and when 'an exploding shell of some type' hit the roof there was 'a tremendous blast.' The 'church attic' (belfry) had been used as a store for explosives.

Obviously the writer of the article had never entered the ruined church or he would have seen the molten mass of the bells at the foot of the tower. A 'tremendous blast' would- have scattered them. In fact, it is obvious that he had never been to Oradour for he maintained that all the men were executed in a field outside the village.

However, the story of women toting arms in Oradour was

also told by an SS ordnance officer, Lieutenant Gerlach who had been captured by the maquis the day before. He said he believed he had been transported through Oradour-sur-Glane where he saw one or two women carrying arms in the street.

Gerlach had driven with six men in three cars to reconnôitre possible billets for the regiment in Nieul. As the accommodation seemed to be insufficient for all of them, he decided to move to the next town, and made the same mistake as Kämpfe's. Although he had been warned of maquis activity in the region, he ordered his driver to race ahead of the others.

Suddenly the road was blocked by a party of armed maquisards who took charge of their car. They were driven for some distance and stopped in a wood. They were forced to get out and moved with their

Colonel (Obersturmbahnführer) **Sylvester Stadler gave Diekmann permission to search Oradour. But did he approve the massacre of all the people?**

captors among the trees where they were made to strip to their underwear.

Gerlach was convinced that were going to be killed. His driver struggled and while the men's attention was concentrated on him Gerlach ran through the wood, with bullets smacking against trees around him. He eventually got out of range and, after wandering a long time, stumbled on the railway line. He followed the line to Limoges where, still in his underwear, he reported to his CO, Colonel Stadler.

Diekmann closely questioned Gerlach who said he saw the village nameplate Oradour-sur-Glane. In the main street, in addition to the armed women, he saw a bakery with the name Boucholle on it. (Boucholle was an Oradour baker). His driver never returned.

By this time Diekmann felt that if the story of a German officer being held prisoner in Oradour was true it must be Kämpfe. He got Stadler's approval for him to go to Oradour as soon as possible to search the place, although Stadler was not convinced by the story and thought Kämpfe might be held elsewhere. If Kämpfe were still alive and held somewhere else Diekmann should try to capture some maquis leaders and use them for negotiation.

An uncorroborated story is that a maquis prisoner held by the Limoges SD (SS security service) was released with a view to finding Kämpfe's captors, offering them 15,000 Reichmarks for his release. Not unnaturally, the man disappeared.

Shortly after 9 a.m., Joachim Kleist, of the Limoges Gestapo, renowned for his brutality, was summoned by Lammerding to the Hôtel Central, accompanied by Eugène Patry, the Gestapo interpreter. Outside was a truck containing four militiamen. They were Pitrud (the leader), Davoine, Tixier and Tomine. Davoine had served in a battalion of *Chasseurs Alpins* in 1939 in the company of Darnand, the chief of the militia. He was a prisoner of war for over two years before he escaped. Unable to return home, he went to Nice where he met Darnand again. At the beginning of 1943, Darnand made him his bodyguard and in May 1944 promoted him a militia inspector concerned with Jewish problems and an auxiliary inspector of the Police Nationale, the office he held in Limoges. These men received orders from Lammerding to help the SS in 'an operation in the region of Saint-Junien'.

Their truck was preceded by a truck carrying a number of soldiers, and was followed by three trucks carrying rations and munitions for Diekmann's men at Saint-Junien.

Diekmann summond the militiamen and Gestapo officers to the Hôtel de la Gare where he presided over a conference in the dining room on the ground floor. He was accompanied by Captain Otto Kahn, the CO of the third company of the battalion, whose men were involved in the massacre, together with other officers. The militiamen, with Patry interpreting, provided local knowledge. The conference lasted just over an hour.

Hôtel de la Gare at Saint-Junien where plans were made for the massacre.

CHAPTER EIGHT

The Motive

It is obvious from the mechanical way in which the raid was carried out that the SS were well briefed about the village which they had never seen before. The information provided by the militiamen is believed to have included the use of an ordnance map.

Towards noon, 120 men of the third company, which had a complement of 180, were told to prepare for action in the afternoon. The militiamen were told they could return to Limoges. One wonders how they felt when they heard how their information had been used. Eight trucks, two armoured tracked vehicles (*Schutzpanzerwagen*) and a motor-cycle were lined up. Armament included four heavy machine-guns, twenty-four light machine-guns and fifteen machine pistols.

The third company were specialists in explosives and incendiary devices. They took what was needed to destroy a large number of houses and asphyxiate people grouped in a large building. The company included many Alsatians who, with the other men, probably did not realise they were to kill far more people than they had ever done before, including hundreds of women and children. As they took their places in the vehicles, they were given a hint that the action was going to be something special. A junior officer, Lieutenant Heinz Barth, passed among them remarking, 'Now you're going to see the blood flow,' and adding, 'Now we'll see what the Alsatians can do.'

The convoy set out at 1.30 p.m. Oradour was only about nine and a half kilometres away (about six miles), but they did not take the direct route. They travelled east on the road that runs parallel to the River Vienne, passing through Saint-Victurnien, then swung north to join the Limoges road shortly before Oradour. This was evidently a tactical move to facilitate the rapid surrounding of the village. The direct route from Saint-Junien enters Oradour halfway up the main street. The convoy would be entering at the southern end.

A halt was called en route and Diekmann, who had been travelling in a commandeered Citröen *deux chevaux* with his adjutant and an Alsatian driver, ordered the officers and NCOs to gather round. They were given a final briefing. It is possible that they were then told they could tell the men no one was to be spared. He may have spoken of a search for Kämpfe and for arms caches but did not expect results. The whole place was to be razed as an impressive lesson to the maquis and their sympathisers. He is believed to have spoken to Stadler on his radio before moving off. He probably told him he was about to enter Oradour. He may also have told him that he planned to execute hostages and burn the village, but it's unlikely that he said he was going to kill every living soul, including hundreds of women and children.

Some facts are known. Kahn who supervised the slaughter, constantly hustled the soldiers to 'get on with it'. There was some taunting of the Alsatians who may soon have realised that they were involved in an action that was larger and more merciless than anything previous. Liquor was widely looted but the killers did not have time to fortify themselves during the operation. They imbibed afterwards and went singing on their way to Nieul. Motivated by blind obedience to orders and fear of the consequences should they show any hesitancy in carrying out the butchery, the men must have worked like automatons, squeezing triggers, changing magazines, hurling grenades and starting fires with petrol they had stolen in Saint-Junien.

Yet it is difficult to imagine the state of mind of the men, particularly if Alsatians were involved, who were ordered to kill the women and children in the church. Were they completely unmoved by the screams and pitiful pleadings ? Did none of them hesitate when they were ordered to fling grenades among the babies in their prams? Hundreds of rounds must have been fired in the church. The salvage team found the floor littered with empty cases, particularly near the main entrance.

Even more ghastly is the thought of men clambering over the bleeding bodies of the women and children to spread straw and faggots, topped by chairs.

Marguerite Rouffanche said she heard screams when the flames started to spread. Some of the victims were still alive. The killers may have realised this when they prepared the pyre but it seems that no effort was made to locate the sufferers and finish them off with pistol shots as they had done with the men. The last cries may have come from the forty-one babies in a side

Major *(Sturmbahnführer) Adolf* Diekmann who conceived and organised the massacre. His superiors described him as an 'open, honest and decent man'.

chapel who had been protected for a while by their sturdy prams.

According to Lieutenant Barth, the only officer of the raiding party to be tried, Diekmann told the officers that Oradour must be razed to the ground, as a punitive measure and to deter the Resistance from further activity. He did not mention a search for

Kämpfe. Towards the end, it seemed as if the officers realised they were doing something so vile that they were afraid to leave a single witness and killed people who might have been spared. The Gestapo's search for survivors was further evidence of the bid to hush things up.

Before summarising the apparent motives for the massacre, it is worth considering what other people have said.

German General von Brodowski, commanding the Clermont-Ferrand region, was said to have been carrying a diary when he was arrested on 26 October 1944. This was his entry for 11 June, 1944:

'In the course of an action on the 10th, Oradour and its environs (31 kms south-west of Limoges) was reduced to ashes.'

The entry for 14 June reads:

'Regarding Oradour – 30 kms south-west of Limoges – a French version has been received. Six hundred people perished. An untersturmführer *of the SS amoured division* Das Reich *had been taken prisoner at Nieul (8 kms north-west of Limoges) and transported to Oradour. He managed to escape. The body of a paymaster class one, bearing traces of handcuffs, was subsequently found. The whole of the male population of Oradour has been shot. The women and children took refuge in the church. The church caught fire. Explosives had been stored in the church. The women and children perished.'*

There is some doubt about the authenticity of the report, but if it is true von Brodowski was apparently referring to Gerlach's capture and escape. The reference to Oradour being south-west of Limoges supports the popular theory that the 'wrong Oradour' was attacked. Oradour-sur-Vayres lies south-west of' Limoges and was reputed to be a centre of maquis activity.

Raymond Carter, in his book *Le Scandale d'Oradour*, supports the 'wrong Oradour' theory. He quotes a former resistance leader who, he says, told him that the maquis attacked a section of *Das Reich* Division near Oradour-sur-Vayres as a reprisal for atrocities committed by the SS elsewhere. There were many casualties on both sides. In revenge, the SS decided to wipe out the village and sent an execution squad to the wrong place.

The killers knew exactly where they were going and why and were helped by people who were well acquainted with the region. They were pressed for time, being considerably delayed in their movement to the Normandy battlefield, and knew

Oradour would be an easy target. They felt it would be a dramatic warning to the Resistance not to carry out further attacks of the kind they had already experienced.

A French historian, not a local man, told the author the real reason for the massacre, which had been hushed up, was that two German motor-cyclists had been found dead, horribly mutilated, in a ditch near Oradour. There is no confirmation of this. Kleist, the Gestapo officer, is reported to have told his associates that hostages were to be taken in Oradour and shot as a reprisal for a 'terrorist' attack on an SS vehicle. The twelve soldiers in it had been taken to Oradour where they were all hanged except an officer who escaped. (The Gerlach story again?)

Two authoratitive books on the history of the *Waffen* SS give the same reason for the massacre. George H Stein, in his book *The Waffen SS, Hitler's Elite Guard at War* (Oxford University Press 1966) says 'As elements of the division (*Das Reich*) passed near the village of Oradour-sur-Glane a French resistance sniper shot and killed an officer.' While in the book *Uniforms, Organisation and History of the Waffen SS* by R J Bender and H P Taylor (published by Bender) we find: 'As the division passed near the village of Oradour-sur-Glane a French sniper shot and killed a captain.'

It is highly unlikely that anyone would fire at an SS convoy near a village knowing that the consequences could be devastating.

An official explanation in *Crimes Ennemis en France* (Archives du Service de Recherche des Crimes de Guerre) states that an SS deserter said his unit had been ambushed by the maquis about fifteen kilometres from Oradour-sur-Glane. Four soldiers were wounded and Diekmann, who was leading them, decided that the next village they came to should suffer reprisals. Who was this deserter, when did he desert and what became of him?

M Chaintron, a former prefect of Haute-Vienne, the department in which Oradour is situated, writes in a preface to *Oradour-sur-Glane, Vision Epouvante*, published by the Association des Familles des Martyrs d'Oradour-sur-Glane, that the object of the slaughter was to terrorise people in the region by a frightful example, with a view to discouraging them from supporting the liberation movement launched by the Resistance, and to illustrate beyond doubt that the Germans were still all-powerful.

This is true. It was the main reason for Lammerding's approval of the raid.

An extrodinary theory in a book entitled *Oradour, Massacre and Aftermath* by Robin Mackness, published in 1988, has provoked anger among the survivors and relatives of the dead because it implies that the people had taken gold bars looted by the SS, which became the reason for the raid.

The basis for this is the account by a man called Raoul, who claimed he was the sole survivor of an ambush by a small group of maquisards in a lane about three kilometres from Oradour the night before. They had attacked a convoy carrying a quantity of gold bars which had been looted by Lammerding, Diekmann and Kämpfe. Raoul claimed that the gold was carried in a truck with other loot and there were armoured vehicles in the convoy, all of which were put out of action with grenades and every German except one was killed. Six young maquisards were also claimed to have been killed.

Raoul said he had buried the gold, which was in thirty boxes, in the early morning and recovered it years later.

Apparently, the German who escaped had told the SS in Limoges about the ambush. Diekmann had a stormy meeting with Lammerding who blamed him for sending the convoy along a minor road with only light protection. They assumed that the gold had been taken to the nearest village, Oradour, and Diekmann had taken the indirect route to the village in the hope of finding some of it among the wreckage of the convoy.

The story is far fetched for the following reasons:

(1) If there had been such an ambush surely it would not have been undisclosed for so long? The destruction of an important German convoy by a small band of maquisards would have been acclaimed by the Resistance and recorded in the Limoges archives. Nothing was said about it during and after the war and no other publication has mentioned it. (The *Daily Mail* sent a journalist to Oradour to investigate, and their two page centre spread was headed 'THE AMBUSH THAT NEVER WAS'.)

(2) It is inconceivable that one man could have buried thirty boxes of gold (the heaviest metal) in daylight, unaided and surrounded by wrecked vehicles when the area was swarming with Germans and farm personnel who would have been on their way to work in that area. And who cleared up the debris

and dealt with the dead? There is no record of such salvage.

(3) The noise of the fighting would certainly have been heard in and around Oradour and the people would have kept their children at home instead of sending them to school.

(4) From all accounts the people were happily contemplating liberation and no one, it seems, had any foreboding. They would have been uneasy and alert had such an incident taken place in their locality.

Diekmann's personal account of the raid was:

'*On 10/6 at 13.30 hours the 1st Battalion of the SS DF (Der Führer) surrounded Oradour. After a search the village was burnt. Munitions were found in almost every house. On 11/6 two companies marched to Nieul-le-Chateau. The terrorists had evacuated the locality during the night. Total casualties: 548 enemy dead, one of our men wounded.*'

Major *(Sturmbannführer)* Otto Weidinger.

Major Weidinger, in his history of the *Der Führer* Regiment, said Diekmann reported to Colonel Stadler, his commanding officer, when he returned to the regimental headquarters in Limoges. He said his men had met with resistance in Oradour but had not found Kämpfe. However, they had come across the bodies of a number of murdered German soldiers during the search and had discovered several arms caches. He said all the men who could be identified as 'terrorists' had been shot. The women and children had been locked in the church which had ammunition in its steeple. This exploded when flames from the burning houses spread to the church and the women and children, who had been put there for their own safety, perished in the blaze. Stadler doubted

Diekmann's story and was deeply shocked when he had the full account of the massacre. He told Diekmann he would be court-martialled and accused him of 'sullying the regiment's name for ever'.

Lammerding approved the killing of the men but saw the killing of the women and children in the church was a crime. He said he would arrange a court martial as soon as circumstances allowed.

It is possible that Diekmann was surprised and humiliated by the dressing down he received from his superiors. The article in *Siegrunen* said he was 'wracked with guilt over the death of the women and children' and vowed he would die in battle. To achieve this, he went into action near Falaise without his helmet and a shell splinter entered his skull. Certainly he did die in this manner but it is highly unlikely that he purposely shed his helmet.

Adolf Diekmann as a Second Lieutenant (*Unterstürmführer*).

The SS Major-General Kurt Meyer, first German war criminal to be condemned to death, (the sentence was later commuted) said Oradour was the only crime committed by the SS, and that it was the action of a single man. He was scheduled to go before a court-martial but died 'a hero's death' before he could he tried.

Lammerding, in a letter to the Bordeaux tribunal in 1953, said Diekmann had 'exceeded his orders.' Oddly, Diekmann was allowed to retain his command of the 1st Battalion of the *Der Führer Regiment*. Although he will go down in history as the man responsible for the massacre, Deikmann's records reveal that his superiors had a high opinion of him. Stadler assessed his character as open, honest and decent, reliable at all times, respected and popular. If this is true, how on earth did he become so debased as to order the killing of 642 people and the destruction of their homes?

The son of a school teacher, Diekmann was born in 1914. He joined the SS in 1933 and in 1936 was a member of an SS Signals Battalion who sent him to an SS officers' school at Bad Tölz in 1937. He became an officer cadet and subsequently an upper cadet officer, joining in September 1938 the *Germania* Regiment which occupied the Sudetenland.

He was appointed an *Unterstürmführer* (second lieutenant) that year. As a platoon leader he distinguished himself when war broke out and was awarded the Iron Cross 2nd Class in November 1939 for his service in Poland. In 1940 he married a doctor named Hedwig Meinde who bore him a son (Ranier Adolf) in March 1942. In May 1940 he was wounded at Saint-Venant in northern France, a bullet passing through a lung. Shortly after his return to duty he received the Iron Cross lst Class. In 1942 as a *Hauptsturmführer* (captain) he was an instructor in tank warfare. Like his friend Kämpfe, he served in Russia before joining the reformed *Das Reich* Division. In April 1944 he became a *Sturmbahnführer* (major) and took charge of the 1st Batallion of the *Der Führer* Regiment. Although his record claims that he had 'above average intelligence' he allowed a ruthless vengeance to take charge of himself when he learnt of Kämpfe's capture. Stadler described him as a 'perfect SS man', which meant he had achieved the standard of heartless brutality instilled in him by his training. It came to excessive heights at Oradour. Did he really 'come to Earth' again after the massacre and suffer repentance for what he had done? It is questionable.

The motive for the massacre and associated actions may now be summarised:

(l) The SS were frustrated and furious over their many clashes with the Resistance during their drive to the north and needed a spectacular show of their power and their determination to stand no more delays.

(2) Kämpfe's disappearance was the last straw and they resolved to fulfill their aim without further delay.

(3) It seems likely that the story of some person or persons currying favour with the SS by relating the rumour of a German officer being held captive in Oradour is true. The party of French militia and Gestapo who travelled from Limoges to Saint-Junien could not be the informers. Their job was to provide knowledge of the locality which might help Diekmann

in the raid he had already planned.

(4) Diekmann may have heard that Oradour-sur-Vayres was a centre of maquis activity and, being loath to have another clash with them, chose to vent his wrath on Oradour-sur-Glane which he believed would be an easy target. Besides Oradour-sur-Vayres was about 20 kilometres south of Saint-Junien and he did not want to go back that way.

(5) Diekmann's fury over the loss of Kämpfe verged on insanity. He was not convinced that Kämpfe was held in Oradour, in fact, he doubted if he was still alive but he used his rescue plan to get Stadler's approval. He had Gerlach's account of his passage through an 'armed' Oradour to support his case.

(6) It is hard to believe that he told the entire assembly of officers and militia at the Hôtel de la Gare that he had decided to kill the whole population, including the women and children, although his decision to employ men who were experts in explosives and the preparation of gas bombs to hit people crowded in a limited space (the church) must have been suspicious.

(7) The SS creed of obedience to orders which turned them into automatons would prevent any of the other officers from criticising any aspect of the plan. Perhaps Diekmann withheld his final 'kill them all' order until the column's halt on the Limoges road when he radioed Stadler to say he was about to enter Oradour, without mentioning his mad desire for revenge.

(8) Diekmann set up a command post in a farmhouse nearby, leaving the immediate operation of the slaughter in the hands of Kahn, CO of the third company whose men were involved. They were ordered to 'get on with it' as soon as he had given the signal.

The deterrent effect of the massacre seems to have been achieved. A Resistance leader is said to have paid a secret visit to the smoking ruins and was so impressed that he advised other leaders not to try to take control of any more towns or villages. A long-planned attack on Limoges by combined maquis was called off. The news of what had happened spread widely, in spite of the ban on press coverage. People were terrified that any stand by maquis in their communities could lead to a similar massacre and thereafter there were a few minor clashes but nothing big. One was near Bellac where a party of

FTP attacked a stationary German truck not realising that it was part of an SS convoy standing nearby. They came under a hail of bullets and five of them were killed.

When the *Das Reich* eventually reached Normandy and went into action it was still a formidable fighting force in spite of their losses en route. They had suffered far fewer casualties than the maquisards. However, in the fighting against the Allied forces they lost about 960 men.

Was the Resistance in any way involved in the Oradour story, apart from the capture of Kämpfe and Gerlach? Colonel Rousselier, the commander of the 12th Military Region of the FFI in Limoges, said,

'There was no engagement of any sort in the Oradour-sur-Glane area. We had no camp, no arms cache, and no explosives anywhere near the village.'

However, a Limoges correspondent, who was in the city at the time, wrote to the author,

'There were maquis with arms around Oradour. A friend of mine was two kilometres from the village with his group of communist partisans.'

It is possible that there were uncoordinated groups in several parts of the area. This correspondent said there were more than a thousand maquis-

Lammerding, commander of *Das Reich*, claimed that Diekmann had exceeded his orders at Oradour. However, he allowed him to retain his command.

133

ards in the vicinity of Oradour at that time and if they had united under a common leader they might have attempted to rescue some of the people. But it is doubtful whether any number of lightly-armed partisans would be prepared to face 120 fully-armed and experienced soldiers with the reputation that *Das Reich* had achieved in its march northwards.

It is unlikely that there was ever any association with the Resistance in Oradour. A plaque fixed to the ruins of the home of the mayor, Doctor Jean Desourteaux and his son Doctor Jacques Desourteaux has been contributed by the Association Amicale des Medecins du Maquis et de la Résistance. If there were arms in the village, no real effort was made to find them. In fact, Lieutenant Barth, at his trial in 1983, said the search lasted only five minutes.

But even if Oradour was a Resistance centre and there had been a number of arms caches, this could never be regarded by civilised people as justification for the slaughter of 642 men, women and children and the destruction of their homes.

CHAPTER NINE

'Justice'

In the years following the end of the War, the Oradour massacre tended to be overshadowed by various international developments. It was even dismissed by some with the popular French comment, *'C'est la guerre.'* But the survivors and the relatives of the victims could not forget, in spite of the 'soft soap' of national recogition in the form of the *Croix de Guerre* for the monument to the dead and the Légion d'Honneur conferred on the village during one of several ministerial visits.

State funds were provided to build a barracks-type village near the ruins and plans were drawn up for 'a magnificent new Oradour'. The ruins were classified as a historic monument and taken over by the Beaux Arts. The dead received the ultimate accolade – *'Morts Pour La France.'* However, the Association des Familles des Martyrs was far from appeased. The members clamoured for the tracing of the guilty and their being brought to trial. This was not easy with the *Das Reich* survivors scattered and hiding in a divided Germany. Seven Germans were arrested and accused of having taken part in the massacre. But what about the rest?

One difficulty was that the law in France, and in certain other countries at that time was that no ex-serviceman could be punished for something he had done on the orders of a superior, however criminal the act might be. It was soon establisbed that men from Alsace-Lorraine had taken part. But how could one accuse anyone from a country which had suffered so much under the Nazi yoke? Altogether, 130,000 young men had been forcibly enrolled in the German forces and 42,000 had been killed or were missing. Those who were conscripted and managed to escape formed the Association of Deserters, Escapees and Forced Recruits. It was this body that rallied to defend the fourteen Alsatians who were eventually added to the list of the men for trial.

A number of men accused of having taken part in the massacres at Tulle and Oradour appeared before tribunals in the decade following the end of the war. The proceedings were confused and generally considered unsatisfactory. In each case the principal offenders were missing and the sentences imposed on those who appeared were considered inadequate and aroused widespread indignation.

There were three successive trials concerning the hanging of the ninety-nine men at Tulle. On 29 March 1949, members of the 95th Security Regiment were charged with killing railwaymen at Tulle on 7 June 1944. There were ten of them, two officers, a sergeant-major and seven corporals. They all claimed to be acting on the orders of their superiors. The officers and the warrant officer were condemned to prison with hard labour and the others were acquitted. The sentences caused an uproar in Tulle, being considered far too lenient.

Of the several men involved in the hangings, only two had been located and were tried on 4 July 1951.They were Major Wulf who headed the first convoy of the *Das Reich* division to enter Tulle and a warrant officer named Hoff who was regarded as the principal hangman. Wulf was condemned to ten years with hard labour and Hoff to life imprisonment. Lammerding and Kowatsch, who could not be traced, were sentenced to death in their absence. The proceedings and sentencing were subsequently considered to be irregular and, on 27 May 1952, Hoff alone appeared before another tribunal. His advocate astonished the court by revealing that Wulf had been released the previous week and returned to Germany. Hoff's sentence was accordingly modified from life imprisonment to five years.

The most important trial took place at Bordeaux in January 1953. It was officially known as 'L'Affaire Kahn et Autres', but to the world it was known as the Oradour trial. It was rocked by politics, punctuated by outbursts and, in the end, none of the accused was executed. The deplorable part of the Bordeaux tribunal was that of the twenty-one accused none was an officer. The highest rank was that of a senior warrant officer.

Of the fourteen Alsatians, two had served in the French Army from 1939-40. Six had deserted from the SS in Normandy and surrendered to the British. They told of the Oradour massacre and, after interrogation by French officers, enlisted in the FFI. Two of them subsequently served with the French Army in Indo-China. Between 1945 and 1948, eight of the Alsatians had been interrogated from time to time as witnesses of the massacre. Between times they carried on their normal civilian occupations in Alsace. It was not until three weeks before the

The accused Alsatians at the Bordeaux tribunal.

opening of the trial that the fourteen Alsatians were arrested and charged under a law of 1948 which created an offence of 'collective responsibility.' One of them was immediately regarded as a traitor. He was a sergeant who had volunteered to serve in the SS. Most of them had been between the ages of 17 and 19 when they took part in the massacre.

As soon as the accusations were announced the people of Alsace-Lorraine protested violently. They maintained that the young men of their country who were acccused were as innocent as the people who had been killed at Oradour. They were all victims of the Nazis. They pointed to what had happened to the young men who had evaded conscription. If they were caught they were shot. In any case, caught or not, their families suffered deportation. They referred to the *Gauleiter* who had been appointed to rule Alsace-Lorraine, Robert Wagner. He had compelled the young men to enlist in the German forces and had been shot for that crime. All the Alsatians who were conscripted, they claimed, were the victims of that evil man and it was utterly unjust to accuse them of actions for which they were not responsible, actions which they could not avoid without losing their lives.

At the time of the trial General Lammerding was believed to be in Düsseldorf in the British zone, and carrying on his old profession of civil engineer. The French government asked the British to extradite him so that he could be brought to the tribunal. It was then reported that he and his wife had left their home for an unknown destination, but neither the British nor the German authorities made any apparent effort to find them. Eventually it became known that they had taken refuge in Schleswig-Holstein. Lammerding was finally traced to Wiesbaden in the American zone. Thereafter interest was lost in him. The British reluctance to extradite Lammerding was based on their decision in 1948 to extradite no one from their zone 'except where a charge of murder could be proved beyond any doubt', and this involved a detailed accusation confirmed by numerous witnesses.

One of the sensations of the Oradour trial was the arrival of a letter from Lammerding in which he claimed that both he and Colonel Stadler (who was also known to be alive at that time) knew nothing of the massacre until it was over. The accused, he said, should be acquitted, because they could not disobey Diekmann's orders and Diekmann himself had 'exceeded his orders.' To prove the authenticity of his letter, Lammerding had his signature witnessed by a solicitor. A number of German newspapers were critical of his behaviour. A Frankfurt paper stated that Herr Lammerding was formerly the chief of a group which claimed to represent the ideals of fidelity and virility. Yet when some of the men he had commanded were in a difficult situation at Bordeaux, surely his place should have been with them? Should not he have hastened to support them?

In 1965 Lammerding came into the news again when he sued a German journalist who had dared to recall, in an article, that he had been condemned to death in France for executing hostages. His accusation reiterated his plea of innocence in the Tulle and Oradour affairs. He sheltered behind dead men, Kowatsch who, he said, was responsible for the Tulle hangings, and Diekmann whose initiative led to the Oradour massacre. It is worth noting that he never accused Kahn who was believed to be alive somewhere in Sweden. His action failed.

In accordance with the custom of that time, the Bordeaux

tribunal was a military one. It was composed of six officers who had been active in the Resistance and a presiding civilian, M Nussy Saint-Saens, a judge of the appeal court at Bordeaux, who managed to keep control of the court despite exceptionally awkward circumstances.

There were sixty-five names on the list of the accused, of whom forty-four, including Kahn, were regarded as *en fuite* (in flight from justice). As soon as the identity of the accused had been established, M Schrekenberger, president of the Bar of Strasbourg, who had been condemned by the Germans to imprisonment with hard labour for his work for the Resistance, referred to the forcible recruitment of the Alsatians as a war crime.

'We cannot accept that these young Alsatians should be linked with the Germans when assessing the guilt of those responsible for the massacre.'

M Nussy Saint-Saens stressed that it was really the Nazi regime that was on trial. Everyone was horrified by the massacre and wondered how it could possibly have happened. His answer, and he would underline it, was that it happened because some beings who had lost all trace of human dignity had been bent on establishing by force a completely materialistic order. It was the blind obedience to the totalitarian state, he asserted, that had brought about this terrible thing.

The president had to curb many demonstrations in the courtroom, principally by the relatives of the dead and the survivors, who sat in a group towards the front of the court. The accommodation was primitive and overcrowded. The accused were divided into two groups, the Germans on one side, the Alsatians on the other. They were bunched up together on wooden benches.

When the indictment was read everyone in the court rose. The bereaved wept. The accused maintained an appearance of indifference. One of the Germans, named Nobbe, admitted having taken part in all the atrocities at Oradour. He pleaded guilty to all the accusations. However, he was proved to be mentally ill and was removed to hospital.

The trial lasted from 12 January to 13 February. There were sixty witnesses for the prosecution. Messrs Broussaudier, Roby, Borie and Hébras, survivors of the shooting in the Laudy barn, gave their story. The sole survivor of the women, Mme

Rouffanche, engendered a great deal of emotion with her testimony and there was much use of handkerchiefs as well as outbursts of indignation.

The men could not identify any of the accused. Not unnaturally, in the heat and terror of the moment, the features of any individual executioner had not lingered in their memories. Besides, the machine-gunners were standing with their backs to the light at the entrance to the barn. In their camouflaged tunics and helmets they all looked alike.

· Armand Senon, who had been immobilised by his fractured leg, described how, from his bedroom window, he saw the round-up of the people on the *Champ de Foire*. M Lamige said about twenty-three people were brought in from the surrounds. He saw the savage beating of a wounded survivor of the 1914-18 war. Mme Coudert and M Lévèque described how they saw the SS convoy approaching the village. M Tarnaud said the village was completely encircled and the soldiers methodically searched the surroundings. The brothers Martial and Maurice Beaubreuil said they saw the first of the trucks pass while they were in hiding. They jumped on their bicycles and dashed towards Les Bordes. They came under fire but were not hit.

Robert Besson and Jacques Garraud described how they climbed a wall to escape. They came under fire and scrambled for shelter among some brambles. They were not found, but a man and two women who had been hiding in a field were spotted by a patrol and shot. M Boissou told how, while fleeing from Les Bordes to another hamlet, by way of a field of corn, he came under machine-gun fire.

M René Hyvernaud said that when night fell he saw a convoy carrying loot pass near the station of Veyrac. The soldiers were singing while one played an accordion and another a mouth organ.

A number of witnesses asked about identification of the accused, said their sole aim that afternoon had been to get out of the way of the soldiers, not to concentrate on their faces. Besides, it was over eight years ago. In any case, they could not understand why they should have to identify any of them. They had been SS soldiers and if they admitted being at Oradour that day, surely that was enough to convict them?

Commissioner Massiéras, who was attached to the information service in Limoges, said he went to the ruins at the

The accused Germans.

request of the regional prefect, on 12 June. At the church he noticed that the windows of the vestry had been broken and there were bullet holes inside. The SS must have fired at the women there, about thirty in all. He visited some of the other execution sites and noticed that the bullet holes in the walls were about the height of the chests or heads of the victims.

Doctor Bapt and Doctor Benech, who accompanied the salvage team, spoke of twisted arms and clenched fists of the dead, evidence of the suffering they had endured before dying. There were numerous fractures of the lower limbs and visible points of impact low down on the walls, from which it might be concluded that many of the victims had been deliberately shot below the waist.

A young priest, the Abbé Touch, who helped with the removal of the corpses from the church, said he found a number of dead children behind the altar. It was as if they had been put there by their mothers, hoping they might be spared.

During the testimony of the prosecution witnesses there was trouble when it was learnt that the French National Assembly had repealed the 1948 Act of 'collective responsibility'. The effect in the courtroom was dramatic. The survivors and many of the bereaved refused to sit down. M Brouillaud, president of the *Association des Familles des Martyrs* addressed the judges. He maintained that, by their action, 350 deputies had weakened the case against the prisoners. The bereaved were afraid the killers might be reprieved. This could not be tolerated. He was ordered to sit down. He refused and was threatened with expulsion from the courtroom. There was general commotion. The Oradour people blocked the exits. The Press joined in the shouting. There was a demonstration outside the court as well, and speeches were made. The mayor of Bordeaux, wearing his tricolour sash, promised that the orphans of Oradour would be adopted by his city, overlooking the fact that nearly all the

Scharführer (sergeant) Boos who was condemned to death.

children had perished in the church.

When the time came for the prisoners to give an account of their roles in the massacre, they said they had forgotten a great deal of what had occurred. Some said that when they were ordered to shoot certain people they aimed to miss. The Alsatians claimed they had been 'bullied' into their actions by the officers and NCOs. Prominent among the latter was Sergeant Georg Boos, the Alsatian who volunteered.

One of the Germans, named Pfeffer, who admitted killing people, said Kahn made him do it. He was among those who herded a group of men into a barn and used his machine-gun on them. He aimed at their chests.

Frenzel, another German, said the officers stood behind the firing squads. He also accused Kahn who, he said, personally took part in killing the wounded.

Lenz, a German warrant officer, said he took no part in the massacre. He said he spent the afternoon walking round the village. But he was contradicted by Boos who said Lenz had taken part in the shooting and had tossed grenades among the women and children in the church. He had also thrown incendiary devices into the houses.

One of the Alsatians, Daul, said they had been told at Saint-Junien that they were going to a town to free Major Kämpfe. He had been a member of a machine-gun crew positioned near a farm outside the village. They had been ordered to prevent people from entering or leaving Oradour. They had turned back a girl on a bicycle who had tried to get into the village, also a woman with a shopping bag and a man who wanted to pick up his tobacco ration. Later a music professor from Limoges (probably M Tournier who was among the dead who were identified) argued with them and they allowed him to go into Oradour to talk to an officer. When Daul went into the village he saw Boos shooting people.

Other prisoners described how Kahn took an active part in the massacre. An Alsatian named Elsässer, said one of the women in the church tried to get out and had shouted to Kahn in German that she was not French and should not be treated like the others. Kahn shot her and shoved her into the flames, saying he wanted no witnesses of what was happening.

Josef Busch (Alsatian) admitted being a member of the execution squad at the Desourteaux garage. He thought some of the victims were still alive when they covered them with brushwood and other material, but he was not sure. He was later sent down to the church to make sure no one escaped. He saw two women approach, asking about their children. Boos and a German soldier shoved them into a barn opposite the church, where a group of men had been killed, and shot them.

Paul Graff, another Alsatian, said he was in a field at the edge of the village with a German and a Russian when they saw two women hiding in a hedge. The women started to scream and they shot them. Their bodies were taken in a barrow to one of the burning houses.

Graff said he was ordered to go to the church and helped to carry brushwood inside. He heaped it on the bodies of the women and children. There was some screaming and groaning. One woman and a child who tried to escape were clubbed to death by a soldier. The church was full of soldiers at the time. They were under orders.

One man, Höchlinger, an Alsatian, claimed that he hid in a hedge outside the village throughout the afternoon and had actually gone to sleep. Raab, a German, told of the deployment of the troops when they entered the village. The first platoon went directly up the main street, while the second and third spread out to surround the village. He denied taking part in any of the executions and claimed he spent the time guarding the trucks.

Albert Ochs, an Alsatian who served in the FFI after deserting in Normandy, said he was conscripted in the SS in early 1944. His brother-in-law refused and was shot. He said a German sergeant named Steger had ordered the men to get all the people out of the houses. Anyone who refused or was incapacitated was to be shot. Ochs said he did not shoot anyone. He saw Steger and another German shoving an elderly woman out of her home. He told them, to leave her alone and Steger shouted, 'Shut up, Alsatian!' They shot her in her own doorway. Ochs said he was hit in the legs by ricochets and taken away for treatment by a medical orderly.

Grienberger (German) said he was in an execution squad but deliberately fired high. He deserted in Normandy.

Only one of the accused showed genuine remorse for what he had done. He was an Alsatian named Antoine Lönner, white-haired and soft spoken. He had been conscripted in the SS in

1944 and the deserted in Normandy. He said he had helped to round up the people in the village on the orders of Sergeant Steger. He had acted as interpreter for Kahn and interrogated Doctor Desourteaux when he arrived in the Champ de Foire. Steger's squad took a party of men to the Denys coach house. Among them was an elderly priest. After the executions, Steger set fire to the building and the squad moved down to the church.

Löhner said he saw Boos shoot two women in the doorway of a barn opposite the church. He himself had carried brushwood into the church. He was still haunted by the screams of the women and children. He saw Boos throw grenades among them. Before the detachment left for Nieul, Kahn distributed wine and spirits. Löhner said he was one of the men who returned to Oradour to bury some of the dead.

The supposed villain of the piece, Sergeant Georg Boos, joined the SS in 1942 and was awarded the Iron Cross Russian Service Medal. He said the Oradour raid was planned by the officers. He just obeyed orders throughout the whole affair. Kahn was 'a hard man'. At Saint-Junien they had been told about the disappearance of Major Kämpfe and had been warned to expect heavy fighting at their destination.

Boos admitted leading the last group of men to execution. He also admitted entering the church but could not clearly remember what happened there. He denied shooting two women in the barn opposite the church. He also denied firing a machine-gun in the church. He maintained that the other accused were saying things about him because they wanted revenge.

He was asked if he went into a bakery and after a long pause said he could not remember. The firebox of a bakery oven in which the remains of an eight-weeks-old baby were found was produced in court. Boos refused to reply to all questions about the incident.

So many of the accused claimed they could not remember what had happened, had fired to miss or were not in the village at the time, that the presiding judge was moved to remark at one stage, 'The court finds it difficult to understand how anyone at all was killed at Oradour.'

The picture that emerged from the prisoners' responses was that of a company of excited, brain-washed, frightened men jumping to obey orders barked by furious, brutal officers and NCOs. The soldiers dashed about in response to commands without having a clear picture of what the exercise was about. When the presiding judge asked if there were any among them who were truly repentant for what they had done only three stood up.

Summing up for the prosecution, Colonel Gourdon spoke of the systematic campaign of terrorism conducted by the *Das Reich* Division of the SS. He gave details of some of the crimes they had committed during their march from the south. The main argument for the defence was that the accused were acting under orders which could not be disobeyed. Rigorous discipline was a standard feature of armed forces, particularly in a time of war, but it had to be within the framework of international law. If the orders were manifestly illegal, if they constituted a serious crime, as at Oradour, a soldier had the right to disobey or he might be considered as guilty as his superiors who gave the orders.

At the Nuremberg trial, said Colonel Gourdon, reference had been made to the conception of obedience. The fact that a soldier claimed he had acted only in obedience to his superiors did not relieve him of all responsibility. He had no right to kill or torture in violation of the international laws of war. Another argument for the defence was that members of the SS could never consider disobedience in any form because they knew they would be shot for it. It was a case of killing to avoid being killed.

However, the behaviour of the soldiers at Oradour went beyond the mere slaughter of innocent people to order. No one could forget the statement by M Bellivier who saw them pounce like wild beasts on a woman who was doing her washing in her garden. Nor that of Mme Démery who saw them jump out of their trucks to run about the village, yelling and laughing as they battered the doors with their rifle butts. Then there was the martial music heard just before the shooting and the soldier who distributed sugar lumps, laughing, while he waited for the order to open fire. Professor Forest, who had tried to get into the burning village to find his sons had been amazed by the attitude of the soldiers. They behaved as if they had been to an enjoyable party.

One could not overlook the fact that the accused had been young men, some still in their teens, and knew only to obey their masters, but they should have taken notice of an example of true courage displayed by the mayor. He had offered himself as a hostage, and later his family too, in the hope of saving his fellow villagers. The whole French nation was in admiration of this man who had shown how fear need not prevent someone from offering his life to save others.

Turning to the Alsatians, Colonel Gourdon said he had only noticed a show of emotion, even tears, among them when the plight of their country under the Nazi occupation had been described. Otherwise they seemed singularly indifferent and unmoved by the accounts of the death of a French village, a village they had helped to exterminate.

'The Germans at Oradour were our enemies,' Colonel Gourdon added, 'but the others were actually Frenchmen and they killed their brothers and sisters.' He called for sentences of hard labour for all of the Alsatians except Sergeant Boos, the volunteer, a fanatic Nazi. He deserved to die. He concluded:

> 'Messieurs les Juges,If you find the accused not guilty it will imply that on 10 June 1944, at Oradour-sur-Glane, in spite of the ruins which the whole world can see, the population was not exterminated nor was the village destroyed.'

The principal defence counsel, the Bâtonnier Moliérac, pleaded that the accused had been young men, robbed of all individuality and personality. Were such men intellectually capable of refusing to obey orders from the SS officers and NCOs in the face of the rest of the company?

He cited Jackson, the US prosecutor at the Nuremberg trial, who had said one could not expect the inferior ranks to ponder on the legality of an order. One had to remember that a soldier had but one function – to obey orders, no matter how sickening might be the outcome.

The accused were not at Oradour to have a conscience, but to carry out the orders they had been given. Every army unit was wrapped inescapably in a mantle of discipline. They submitted to orders and to a certain intellectual superiority in those who gave them. They were, in fact, nothing more than an execution squad in both senses of the expression. The accused did not feel they were guilty. They saw themselves as trapped beasts and really didn't know how they could have avoided doing the things of which they were accused. They would have had to be superhuman.

The trial, he went on, was basically that of a totalitarian regime. The chief culprits, many of whom were still alive, could not be brought before them that day, so their dupes, their first victims, were made answerable.

When the time came to review the history of the period, the supreme head of the Nazi regime would be seen to bear responsibility not only for the victims such as those at Oradour but also for the men who carried out his commands. 'It was he who put these men in uniform,' he concluded. ' It was he who held them in a vice of discipline and, after blacking out their intellect, led them by degrees to be involved in the most appalling bestialities.'

A surprise witness for the defence was an Alsatian school teacher, a sister of Odile and Emile Neumeyer, who were among the victims. She said she could not blame her compatriots who took part in the massacre because they had been forcibly recruited and acted under extreme duress.

M de Guardia, defending the Germans, pointed out that many of them, like the Alsatians, had been forced to join the SS. Was it possible for any man in the SS to refuse to execute an order, although it might seem to be a flagrant violation of the laws of war? If he obeyed, he was guilty of such a violation, and if he disobeyed he was guilty in the eyes of his superiors and would suffer the consequences. It seemed that the Germans at Oradour, being human, chose the easy way out. They obeyed because the punishment for disobedience was certain and almost immediate. The military code of many nations approved the death sentence for refusal to obey an order when faced with the enemy.

M de Guardia said a soldier might only appear before a tribunal if his side lost the war. If the commanders of the victorious as well as the defeated forces were to appear before a tribunal composed of victors, vanquished and neutrals, the International Red Cross could open a dossier of terrible crimes. It would reveal the barbarity not only of those involved in the Oradour massacre and the concentration camps, but also those responsible for Katyn, Hiroshima, Hamburg and Dresden for example. Masks would fall and the world would be horrified to see that there were certain strange resemblances between the behaviour of the chiefs on both sides. Then, how many of them would be freed of guilt?

Aerial view of the ruins.

The magistrates retired to consider their verdict on 12 February at 5 p.m. and returned to the courtroom at 2 p.m. the next day.

Of the Germans, Lenz, the warrant officer, was sentenced to death. One of them, Degenhardt, was acquitted and the others were sentenced to terms of imprisonment varying from ten to twelve years most with hard labour. Forty-two other Germans, tried in their absence, were sentenced to death. Among the Alsatians, Boos was sentenced to death, nine others to prison with hard labour and the remaining four to prison. No sentence exceeded eight years.

When the sentences were announced there was a great outburst of indignation throughout France. They were considered utterly inadequate for such a terrible crime. There was a protest march through Limoges in which 50,000 people are said to have taken part. Posters were displayed and banners carried displaying: WE WILL NOT ACCEPT THE VERDICT.

On the other hand, the people of Alsace-Lorraine went into mourning over the injustice of the sentences on their countrymen. They were too severe. The mayors of all the towns in Alsace walked in silent procession past the war memorial in Strasbourg. The Bishop of Strasbourg advocated the quashing of the sentences. Meanwhile in Paris the legislature discussed an amnesty proposal. On 19 February the amnesty law was passed by 319 votes to 211, with 88 abstaining. The Upper House gave approval by 176 votes to 79.

The sentenced Alsatians, with the exception of Boos, were rapatriated in secret. Five of the seven Germans were also sent home, their sentences being less than the eight years they had been detained awaiting trail. In 1954 the two men who were sentenced to death had their sentences commuted to hard labour.

Oradour was outraged. The mayor removed the Croix de Guerre from the *mairie* in the new village and the president of the *Association des Familles des Martyrs* removed the Légion d'Honneur from the cemetery. At the main entrance to the ruins two notice boards were erected. One bore the names and addresses of the Alsatians who had been sentenced and the part that each man was said to have taken in the massacre. The other listed the parliamentarians who had voted for the amnesty.

The list of Alsatians was headed: 'The monsters listed here took part in the murder of 642 inhabitants of Oradour-sur-Glane. These are their names and the crimes they committed.' The end of the list was inscribed,

'Thanks to the amnesty law these criminals are free.'

The parliamentarians' list was headed: 'These 319 deputies pardoned the SS monsters who murdered, burnt and pillaged in Oradour-sur-Glane.'

A list of names followed. Then came:

'These senators confirmed the deputies' vote....', followed by more names.

The boards remained there until 1966.

CHAPTER TEN

The Only Officer

After the war the East Germans created a special force whose job was to search for war criminals and, between the end of the war and 1981, they caught 12,867. The last one to be hanged was in 1970 after which the death sentence was abolished and life imprisonment became the ultimate punishment.

On 14 July 1981 they arrested the 12,868th who was among their biggest catches. He was Heinz Barth, a former lieutenant in the 1st Battalion of the *Der Führer* Regiment of the *Das Reich 2nd Panzerdivision Waffen* SS. He was the man who told the soldiers before they set out to sack Oradour, 'Today you are going to see the blood flow.' He was the only officer of the division concerned with the massacre to be brought to trial. He was among those condemned in their absence by the Bordeaux tribunal.

The extraordinary thing was that he had been living in his home town Gransee, on the edge of a lake, under his own name ever since he returned openly to Germany in 1945, handicapped by the loss of a leg in Normandy. He had escaped detection for nearly forty years because he had faked his service record. An analysis of records eventually trapped him. Barth was kept in custody for two years. His trial in East Berlin opened on 25 May 1983. It was a show trial, lasting ten days, with full television coverage and was attended by journalists from many countries.

Prior to the hearing, the presiding judge, Herr Heinz Hugot, had written to the state prosecutor in Limoges asking for the attendance of survivors of the massacre. Five undertook the journey – Maurice Beaubreuil, Martial Machefer, Yvon Roby, Jean-Marcel Darthout and Robert Hébras. A request was also sent to West Germany for men who had appeared at Bordeaux. The Germans named were Daul, Molinger, Boos, Frenzel and Okrent. Two Alsatians who had been critical of Barth's ruthless behaviour at Gradour, Graff and Elsässer, were also summoned. An odd appeal was sent by Mme Wirtwaz, a relative of Kahn, though how she could provide reliable testimony about Barth was not disclosed. Anyway, none of these people appeared.

Barth came into the courtroom leaning heavily on a stick and

Barth was charged with taking part in the killing of 92 people at Lidice, Czechoslovakia in 1942 as a reprisal for the assassination of Reinhard Heydrich (pictured right).

Above: All males in the village were shot and (below) all trace of the village was obliterated.

looking much older than 62. The walls were lined with maps of France, Haute-Vienne and Oradour.

Apart from the participation in the massacre of 642 people at Oradour, Barth was charged with taking part in the killing of 92 people at Lidice, Czechoslovakia, in 1942 as a reprisal for the assassination of Reinhard Heydrich, the SS general who controlled that country. He admitted volunteering for three firing squads and standing guard for a fourth. He had been a member of an SS police squad.

Barth was questioned about the preparation for the Oradour massacre. He said about a dozen officers attended the conference at the Hôtel de la Gare in Saint-Junien. Diekmann told them that Oradour must be razed to the ground as a punitive measure and to discourage further Resistance activity.

'Our orders were to spare nobody', he said. 'If I had not obeyed I would have been put before a court martial.' He indicated on the map the route the convoy had taken. His section halted at the river bridge before going slowly up the main street. Men were dropped off to surround the village. There were few people in the street, apart from a small crowd outside a bistro:

> 'We were armed with machine-guns and rifles, I had a machine-pistol and an automatic. In accordance with the plans I told the NCOs to arrange the surrounding of the village in such a way that every man could see another and was within earshot. My job was to ensure that this was satisfactorily completed.'

Barth said he had been ordered to block all the exits from Oradour and to shoot anyone trying to get out. When the encirclement was completed, he said, he went to get the people out of their houses and herd them to the *Champ de Foire*.

'We had orders to kill anyone who couldn't or wouldn't leave their homes,' he said. Asked if he remembered ordering the execution of an elderly man in his bed, Barth said he couldn't remember but he may have done. He was told to search the houses for arms. The presiding judge: 'How long did this search last?

Barth: 'About five minutes.'

The President: 'Do you think an experienced policeman could have done the job properly in so short a time?'

Barth: 'No.'

The President: 'What did you find?'

Barth: 'Nothing.'

Barth said that, so far as he knew, no arms or munitions of any kind were found in the village. The president: 'How did the people react?' Barth: 'They were very frightened. We ordered them out of their houses, shoving and insulting them. We formed them into small groups for escorting to the *Champ de Foire*. We knocked before entering each house.'

The President: ' What do you mean by 'Knocked'?'

Barth said : 'We used rifle butts.'

The President: 'The searching of the houses was only a pretext, wasn't it? You knew everyone was to be killed.'

Barth: 'No.'

The President pointed out that this was contrary to his previous statement. He said he had been told that the whole population of Oradour was to be exterminated.

Barth: 'Oradour was only an incident in the march of the *Das Reich* towards Normandy.'

Asked how many people he conducted to the *Champ de Foire*, Barth said he had not counted them but he had probably dealt with around 150. The round-up was completed in half an hour.

The President: 'The orders you received were quite clear?'

Barth: 'Yes. We had to kill everybody, even the children.'

The President: 'What did you do next?'

Barth: 'My group had the job of fetching the children from the schools.' He was next ordered to go to a 'sort of barn or garage' to execute a number of men. The men were inside with the soldiers standing facing them. There were no windows. The men could not escape. They were lined up in two rows. He thought there were about twenty of them, aged between about 25 and 40.

The President: 'Did these men ask what had happened to their wives and children?'

Barth: 'No.'

Barth said he had to await a signal which would ensure that all the executions took place at the same time.

The President: 'What was the signal?'

Barth: 'An explosion. As soon as I heard it I cried, "Fire!" and I and the men with me opened up. I fired two bursts with my machine-pistol of about twelve to fourteen rounds. I aimed at the men's chests.' Pressed to describe his feelings at the time Barth showed his first signs of emotion. He recalled the men's wordless terror and wept as he said in a barely audible voice, 'It is difficult for me to talk about this.'

The president: 'Were there any survivors?'

Barth: 'I don't know. I think they were all dead. When we had finished firing we shut the doors. That part of the operation was finished for me. My next job was to burn the village.'

On his way back to the trucks that had brought them, Barth walked past the church where he knew the women and children were to be executed. He heard moans and saw flames at the windows.

'Is it possible that the women and children were being burnt to death?' asked the President.

Barth: 'I don't know. I had nothing to do with the killings in the church. That was another group.'

The President: 'Did it ever occur to you that such acts were in contravention of the laws of war?'

Barth: 'I had my orders and I obeyed them. It all seemed to me to be part of war. And there was this new front in Normandy to be taken into account. I thought it was essential to wage war as rigorously as possible.'

The President: 'Didn't you have any qualms about your orders?'

Barth: 'No. They were part of war.'

Asked what he had done about the bodies of the men he had killed, Barth said he had not thought any more about them. He knew they would be burnt with the village. He claimed there was no difference in attitude between the Germans and the Alsatians. They all did their duty.

'The population had been condemned in advance,' he said, 'and there was no need to give them any explanation for our action. A man who spoke a little German came to me. He wanted to make me understand he had been working for us. I went to find Kahn to ask what I should do with him. "Kill him" said Kahn, "and hurry up. He's seen too much already."'

Barth said the blame for what they had done could be attributed to the maquis. 'But it was a one-sided action,' said the president. 'There was no retaliation by the French.' Barth said the officers got together when it was all over and they were instructed to tell everyone that they had found arms and ammunition in the village.

The President said: 'That was a lie. What you did was an act

155

of terrorism, pure and simple, wasn't it?'

Barth replied : 'Yes.'

When it came to the turn of the Oradour survivors to give evidence, Robert Hébras (58) said he was about 19 at the time of the massacre. He lost his mother and two sisters.

'About forty to forty-five of us were ordered into a barn,' he said. 'Five soldiers with machine-guns faced us. When they started firing we all fell in a heap. I was at the bottom and was only slightly wounded.'

Jean-Marcel Darthout (59) said, 'I was lucky to be one of the first to drop down. Others fell on top of me. The soldiers came to give us the *coup de grace*. They shot a friend who was on me.'

Maurice Beaubreuil (59) told how he hid under the floorboards in his aunt's kitchen when he saw the SS men coming along the street. When the house started to burn he fled into the garden and saw smoke belching from the tower of the church. The steeple suddenly twisted and fell. The screams he had heard from the church seemed to carry on after the fall of the steeple. They seemed to be screams of pain.

Marguerite Rouffanche, who was then 84 years old, was too old and infirm to make the journey but sent a written statement. She spoke of the heart-rendering cries as the women were separated from the men and forced to go into the church. She

Heinz Barth at his trial in East Berlin in 1983 and, right, as a young second lieutenant (*Untersturmführer*).

described how she was struck by bullets as she escaped from the burning church. Her right arm and leg were crippled.

A surprise feature of the trial was a reference to a letter from Otto Kahn which had been received by the East German Authorities in 1962 when they were investigating the case of Lammerding. Kahn had written that he had tried to dissuade the men from committing some of the atrocities but Barth had insisted that the orders must be carried out to the letter.

In his summing up Herr Horst Busse quoted a clause in the German military code of 10 October 1940. Barth had claimed that his superiors had demanded blind obedience to orders and he could not hesitate to carry them out. However, according to the code, obedience in carrying out a criminal act did not exclude the perpetrator from blame, if he was aware of the nature of the act. Two German experts on criminal acts in war, Alfred Spiesz, public prosecutor of the court of Wippertal, and Adalbert Rükel, chief of the department involved in the search for war criminals in East Germany, had stated that during the Second World War no German soldier had been condemned for invoking Article 47 of the military code, which allowed a soldier to refuse to obey an order if it involved an act that was undoubtedly criminal.

At Treblinka concentration camp an SS NCO had ordered a soldier to kill one of the inmates, a Jew. The soldier had invoked Article 47 and the NCO had dismissed him. A number of soldiers ordered to carry out the slaughter of 780 Russian prisoners, by means of a bullet in the back, had said the order was contrary to the Geneva Convention regarding the treatment of prisoners of war. The officer who gave the order was furious and told them they were cowards, but he allowed them to retire and attend to other duties. (Needless to say, another squad carried out the executions). Apparently none of the men involved at Oradour had thought of invoking the laws of war.

Herr Busse recalled Barth's career from the executions in Czechoslovakia to the extermination of Oradour.

'We are not trying this man solely on the number of murders he committed,' he said, 'but also on the fact that, in full knowledge of the criminality of what he had been ordered to do, he committed and helped to commit bestial crimes against humanity.' He regretted the necessity of summoning the men who had escaped and causing them to relive the horror they had experienced while facing one of the killers of their people. Their presence in East Berlin was a symbol of East Germany's continued fight against fascism at a time when other countries were allowing ideologies destructive to humanity to breed in their midst.

Although it was nearly forty years after the event the men's testimony was clear and confirmed the case for the prosecution. Herr Busse demanded a sentence of life imprisonment. Barth should be excluded from socialist society and deprived of his civil rights for ever.

The defending council, Herr Friedrich Wolf, pleaded for a lenient view of his client; As a credulous young man who fervently believed in Hitler, Barth had been 'caught up' in the guilt of his people. His crimes should be viewed in the light of the collective crimes of that era. At the age of 12, in common with thirteen million other young Germans, he was enrolled in the Hitler Youth Movement. The entire mental outlook of these youths had been moulded by the Nazis for their benefit. Barth had openly returned to Germany in 1945 to start a new life. He had been a good father and an honest citizen. At the time of his arrest he held a responsible post as a textile buyer for Konsum, a co-operative in Gransee.

'We are dealing with a life that has been twice as long since the act as before it. I am not asking you to forget or defend the fascist regime this man served,' he added, 'but to think of Barth as a man instead of an SS executioner. A lighter sentence would not be contrary to the objectives of the court.'

After hearing his advocate, Barth was invited to return to the witness stand where, leaning heavily on his stick and with tears on his cheeks, he exclaimed:

> 'I am ashamed that as a young man I took part in these operations in occupied countries and I hope such things can never happen again. Politicians should see to it that such things can never happen again.'

Barth was sentenced to spend the rest of his life in an East German jail, but was released in 1997 because of his age (78), his health and his repentance. He would continue to receive a pension awarded to a war invalid.

CONCLUSIONS

Considered in relation to other massacres in the Second World War, Oradour may seem to be a minor affair. When one thinks of Hiroshima, Dresden, Katyn, the concentration camps, and the massive carnage and destruction in Russia, Oradour may not seem so terrible. It might be compared with Lidice, the death of a single man being the spark for the slaughter in each case, but in Lidice all the men were shot while the women were sent to concentration camps and the children to an unknown destination. In Oradour the women and children were shot and burnt in the church, traditionally supposed to be a place of sanctuary. Lidice was virtually wiped off the map, not a single building being left standing. Oradour was left as a ghastly ruin, testifying to the world in a more impressive manner the dreadful things that happened there.

It is difficult for most of us today to conceive what must have been in the minds of the SS murderers. Barth appears to have been unmoved at the time of the killings he carried out at both Lidice and Oradour. It was all part of the war to him. When he had shed the uniform of an SS officer, blindly obedient to orders he received from his superiors, he became a good citizen and father. He killed according to 'orders' – that word which has been responsible for millions of unnecessary deaths throughout history. Friend and foe in many a battle would gladly have stopped fighting each other and shaken hands had it not been for 'orders.' The unofficial Chistmas truce in the trenches of the First World War was a typical example of the lunacy of 'orders.' The men were ordered to start killing each other again after exchanging pleasantries in No Man's Land.

It could be argued that the airman who presses the bomb release resulting in the extermination of a large number of innocent women and children, not to mention the men, is as guilty as the SS soldier who butchered the people of Oradour. The difference lies in consciousness of the crime. In Oradour the killing of 642 men, women and children was done by men who saw and heard at close quarters the effect of their actions. Phosphorous bombs dropped on Hamburg and napalm dropped on Vietnam caused the death of thousands in a similarly agonising form to that meted out by the SS at Oradour. Did the airmen ponder on the effect on human flesh of their missiles? They probably hoped they were destroying military targets or killing soldiers of the other side, shutting out of their minds any pictures of people running about screaming, their clothes and hair on fire as a result of the incendiaries and exsplosives dropped on them.

Some of the concentration camps have been preserved with their ghastly apparatus as memorials of the horrors that were carried out there. However, Belsen, the only one I have visited, seemed more like a pleasant public park than a scene of indescribable cruelty. True, one is appalled by the huge mounds labelled to the effect that several thousand people are buried under each of them, and there are reminders of the awful scenes witnessed at the time of the liberation through photographs in a museum at the entrance. But the impact is far removed from that of Oradour. The others, with their gas chambers and ovens, still visible, are undoubtedly more shocking. But these places were specifically designed execution sites, unlike Oradour which was converted in the space of a few hours from a pleasant, populated village to a shocking, smoking place of execution containing the stinking remains of the victims.

Why keep Oradour as an interesting ruin when most of the war-shattered places have been rebuilt?

English-born Raymond Carter, in his book *Le Scandale d'Oradour*, argues against the preservation of the ruins. Here are some of his points:

(1) One does not perpetuate the memory of a cancer victim with a picture on his tomb of his cancer and a description of his agony.

(2) The dead would not have wished for the ruins of their homes to be kept as showpieces. The ruins have been officially preserved under the label 'historic site' and attracts visitors, particularly during the holiday season.

(3) The children of Oradour would have preferred that other children should play and enjoy life where they did before their moments of terror ended their existence.

(4) After the war the Germans offered to rebuild the village. The offer was refused.

(5) When one visits the ruins it is not to pay homage to the dead but rather to examine the detailed evidence of the sadistic behaviour of the SS.

(6) The ruins keep alive hatred for the Germans which should be forgotten in view of the current Franco-German relations. Many French towns and villages are twinned with German places.

(7) The few survivors who live in the new village feel that the government has expelled them from their homes. They should have been rebuilt and they should have been allowed to return. They feel their roots are in the old village and not in the new one. If they had been rehoused at a distance from the ruins this feeling might not be so strong but they are daily faced with the pathetic reminder of their former existence.

There is much sense in what Raymond Carter says. Analysing my own feelings, I doubt whether I should have made the long journey just to see a memorial in a rebuilt village. The ruins are a unique showpiece, which can arouse feelings of enormous pity and horror. One walks in reverence (or at least one should) in a place which is really one vast cemetery.

I have visited war cemeteries in France, Germany and the Far East. The Singapore one is the most impressive I have seen, particularly during the daily downpour when the whole place seemed to be weeping. Yet such places cannot be compared with Oradour. The neatness of row upon row of identical headstones numbs any shock effect, although one is taken aback by the numbers involved.

Oradour presents only too clearly the full story of the deaths of 642 people. One might get a similar effect in a war cemetery if it were littered with the carcases of tanks, aircraft, etc, each labelled, 'Ten men died here... Six men burnt alive in this...' The ruins must surely keep alive hatred against the men who carried out the massacre and, by association, with Germany. Many of the inscriptions on the tombs name the killers as Germans, overlooking the Alsatians, while others call them Nazis, a less definite association in the eyes of the rising generation.

Tulle and other scenes of atrocities carried out by the *Das Reich* Division during their march to the north have nothing like Oradour to show, so their stories tend to be forgotten. Oradour has earned an international reputation.

I can appreciate the feelings of survivors who were rehoused near the ruins of their former homes because the old village is so much more attractive than the new one. The ruins may not be widely advertised as a tourist attraction but it would be surprising if Oradour is not featured in the itinerary of many coach trips. The French government may be criticised for preserving the corpse, for perpetuating the memory of the crime. The ruins are surrounded by a wall, kept in good order, and the entrances are locked at night. But the ravages of the weather are inevitably taking their toll. One wonders how they will look in, say, fifty years' time. Will efforts be made to prop the crumbling walls? Most of the rusty utensils and other household goods on show have disintegrated and some may be lifted by souvenir hunters. The wall should not be difficult to scale and a night patrol is unlikely. Visitors may find that the horror of the occasion has gone. It is too long ago. Like Pompeii, it is cold history. In the church the guide may call for a minute's silence in reverence to the women and children who died there but the people may dutifully obey without feeling anything much.

I firmly believe that the old village should have been rebuilt, with only the church kept in ruins as a stark memorial.

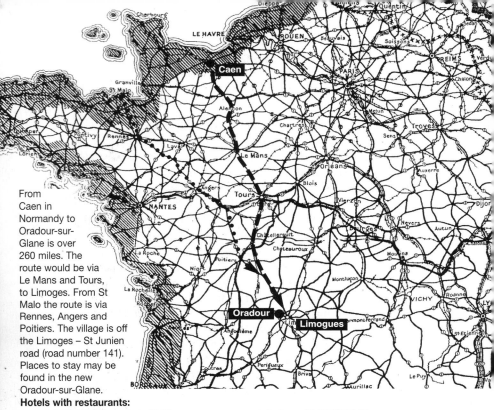

From Caen in Normandy to Oradour-sur-Glane is over 260 miles. The route would be via Le Mans and Tours, to Limoges. From St Malo the route is via Rennes, Angers and Poitiers. The village is off the Limoges – St Junien road (road number 141). Places to stay may be found in the new Oradour-sur-Glane.

Hotels with restaurants:

LA GLANE, Place de la Mairie,	telephone 05.55.03.10.43
LE MILFORD, Av. du 10 Juin,	telephone 05.55.03.10.35
AU BON ACCUEIL, Place de la Mairie,	telephone 05.55.03.26.56
BAR BRASSERIE LE CENTRAL, Av. du 10 Juin,	telephone 05.55.03.14.18

The *Centre de la Mémoire* was opened in April 1999. It is open every day from 9 a.m. to 5 p.m. in winter and until 7 p.m. in summer.

APPENDIX

The Dead

The list of the dead is divided into two parts. The first, totalling fifty-two, comprises the people who could be identified. The second has 585 names. These were the people whose remains were mutilated and burnt to such an extent that identification was impossible. The two lists make a total of 637. Five more names were subsequently added. They were people who had disappeared and were assumed to be in Oradour at the time. The domicile of each person is where he or she was living at the time, so that refugees who had arrived some time earlier are treated as residents. Some of the refugees can be identified by their names, e.g. Espinoza, Lorente, Masachs, Serano (Spanish), Kanzler, Neumeyer (Alsatian).

One pities the Texier children aged four, two and one, respectively, whose Christian names were not known. Also the anonymous, 'M Picat's servant.' Monsieur Picat himself is the only one in the list bearing the title of 'businessman'. Many of the people are described as horticulturists or market gardeners. The SS were probably told of this by their local informers and included tracked vehicles in their convoy to run over the fields and capture the workers. Other rural occupations are blacksmith, wheelwright, sabot maker, well digger, roadman and pedlar. Many of the women were glovemakers probably on contract work in their homes for a firm in Saint Junien the glove-making centre. Yvonne Brandy is described as 'station master' and one can only assume she was in charge of the tiny tramway station. The Milord family were mainly associated with the hotel trade and their name lives on in a hotel in the new village. The list of occupations is incomplete. Presumably many were not known when the list was compiled, but most without occupation were old people and children.

It will be noticed how whole families were wiped out – father, mother, children and grandparents. There are, for instance, eighteen Bardets and twelve Thomases.

List Of Bodies Of People Who Could Be Identified

Name	Occupation	Born	Domicile
ALIOTT1 Christiane		1940	Oradour
AVRIL Michel	Timber merchant	1907	Oradour
BARDET Léonard		1880	Oradour
BESSON Guillaume	Fabric Salesman	1882	Oradour
CHALARD Marcelin	Electrician	1888	Limoges
CHABAUDON Maurice		1914	Limoges
CHAPELOT Louis-Léonard		1900	Oradour
COURIVAUD Maurice	Butcher	1920	La Tuilière-des-Bordes
D'ALBOIS Pierre		1923	Orleans
DALSTEIN Octavie		1887	Oradour
DESBORDES Marie	Horticulturist	1901	Oradour
DESOURTEAUX Jean Doctor	(Mayor)	1872	Oradour
DEVOYON Françoise		1866	Oradour
DUPIC Léonard		1867	Oradour
DUVERNAY François	Farmer	1898	Oradour
FOUSSAT Marie-Léon Miller		1905	Oradour
HYVERNAUDGermaine-Marie	Horticulturist	1903	Oradour
HYVERNAUD Marcel		1936	Oradour
JOYEUX Antonin	Carpenter	1904	Oradour
JOYEUX Henriette		1921	Soudanas
JOYEUX René		1943	Soudanas
JACOBOWICZ Sarah		1929	Oradour
JACKOW Jean		1905	Oradour
LACHAUD Léonard		1872	Oradour (Les Bordes)
LACROIX Jean	Horticulturist	1909	Oradour
LAVERGNE Jean-Baptiste		1902	Limoges
LAVERGNE Jean		1926	Limoges
MILORD François		1915	Lyons
MILORD Hélène	Office worker	1917	Limoges
MIRABLON Albert		1909	Oradour (Le Mas-Férat)
MOREAU Lucien		1911	Limoges
MOREAU Pierre		1882	Oradour
MORLIERAS Lucien	Hairdresser	1902	Oradour
NICOLAS Jean-Babtiste		1884	Oradour
PEYROULET Marcel-Léon		1911	La Betoulle
PINEDE Robert		1899	Oradour
POUTARAUD Pierre-Henri	Garagist	1911	Oradour
RAYMOND Pierre	Horticulturist	1873	Oradour (Valeix)
RAYNAUD Henri-Pierre		1909	Oradour
ROUMY Jean		1896	Oradour
SADRY Jean		1932	Oradour (Le Repaire)
TESSAUD Jean		1890	St Junien
THOMAS Georges		1930	Oradour (Les Bordes)
THOMAS Marguerite		1898	Oradour
THOMAS Marcelin	Baker	1892	Oradour
THOMAS Raymond		1932	Oradour (Les Bordes)
TOURNIER Jean-Baptiste		1893	Oradour
TROUILLAUD Catherine-Marie		1890	Oradour
VALENTIN Jean		1884	Oradour
VIALETTE Daniele		1941	Oradour
VIALETTE Michele		1939	Oradour
VILLOUTREIX Henri		1899	Chez-Garderie

LIST OF PEOPLE PRESUMED DEAD BUT WHOSE REMAINS COULD NOT BE IDENTIFIED

Name	Occupation	Born	Domicile
AIMOND Monique		1932	Paris
ALAMONE Marie-Louise	Servant	1926	Oradour
ALIOTTI Cléa		1921	Oradour
ALIOTTI Félix		1915	Oradour
ALIOTTI Marie		1942	Oradour
ALIOTTI Michele		1944	Oradour
ANDRIEUX Marie		1863	Oradour (Les Brandes)
ARNAUD Monique		1935	Oradour (Les Bordes)
AVRIL Adrienne		1914	Oradour
AVRIL Georges		1943	Oradour
AVRIL Marie	Hotelier	1879	Oradour
BALLOT Aime		1932	Oradour
BALLOT André	Solicitor's clerk	1928	Oradour
BALLOT Jean	Mason	1879	Oradour
BARATAUD Marguerite		1896	Oradour (Les Bordes)
BARDET André	Carpenter	1924	Oradour
BARDET André		1940	Oradour
BARDET Arsène		1935	Oradour
BARDET Arthur	Horticulturist	1910	Oradour
BARDET Catherine		1908	Oradour
BARDET Daniel		1938	Oradour (Les Brandes)
BARDET Denise	Teacher	1920	La Grange-de-Boeil
BARDET Giséle		1926	Oradour (Les Brandes)
BARDET Hubert		1937	Oradour
BARDET Louis	Carpenter	1902	Oradour
BARDET Marie	Glovemaker	1887	Oradour
BARDET Marie		1899	Oradour
BARDET Marie-Claire		1888	Oradour
BARDET Marie-Louise		1911	Oradour
BARDET René		1944	Oradour
BARDET Robert		1931	Oradour
BARDET Yvonne	Glovemaker	1913	Oradour
BARNY Lucien		1938	Oradour (Mazenty)
BARRIERE Marcel	Mechanic	1923	Limoges
BARTHELEMY Alfred	Painter	1887	Oradour
BARTHELEMY Emilie		1869	Oradour
BARTHELEMY Roger	Student	1925	Oradour
BASSEN Marie		1886	Oradour
BEAU Jean	Servant	1882	Cieux
BEAU Joseph	Merchant	1870	Oradour
BEAUBREUIL Emile	Carpenter	1898	Oradour
BEAUDET Angéle	Glovemaker	1921	Oradour
BEAUDET Jean	Cement maker	1887	Oradour
BEAUDET Marie	Glovemaker	1896	Oradour
BEAULIEU Elisa		1894	Oradour
BEAULIEU J-B	Blacksmith	1884	Oradour
BELIVIER A1ice	Horticulturist	1923	Oradour (Les Brégères)
BELIVIER Andre	Horticulturist	1892	Oradour (Les Brégères)
BELIVIER Angele	Horticulturist	1901	Oradour (Les Brégères)
BELIVIER Anne	Horticulturist	1866	Oradour (Les Brégères)

BELIVIER Marie-Louise	Horticulturist	1930	Oradour (Les Brégères)
BERGERON Jules		1875	St Venant
BERGMAN Joseph		1917	Oradour
BERGMAN Marie		1916	Oradour
BERGMAN Serge		1935	Oradour
BERTAND Françoise		1930	Oradour
BESSON Marguerite		1889	Oradour
BEYNE Claudine		1937	Oradour
BICHAUD Jean	Tailor	1891	Limoges
BICHAUD Jean		1934	Oradour (Les Trois Arbres)
BICHAUD Leonard	Roadman	1897	Limoges
BICHAUD Marie	Glovemaker	1901	Limoges
BICHAUD Pierre	Tailor	1934	Limoges
BICHAUD Yvette	Dressmaker	1920	Oradour
BINET Andrée	Teacher	1914	Oradour
BINET Jean	Technician	1910	Limoges
BINET Jean-Pierre		1937	Oradour
BLANDIN Charles		1886	Oradour
BLANDIN Marguerite		1889	Oradour
BOIS Madelaine		1935	Oradour (Orbagnac)
BOISSON Jeanne		1933	Oradour
BOISSON Marie	Horticulturist	1899	Oradour
BONNET Madeleine	Servant	1926	Oradour
BONNET Marie		1934	Oradour (Les Bordes)
BORDENAVE Jean	Pedlar	1922	Oradour
BOSSAVIE Héléne		1933	Oradour (Le Mas-du-Puy)
BOUCHOLLE Gabrielle		1906	Oradour
BOUCHOLLE Henri	Student	1926	Oradour
BOUCHOLLE Léopold	Baker	1899	Oradour
BOUCHOLLE Roger		1929	Oradour
BOULESTEIX Claude		1937	Oradour
BOULESTEIX Christiane		1931	Oradour
BOULESTEIX Léonie	Housekeeper	1907	Oradour
BOULESTIN Lucien		1936	Oradour (Orbagnac)
BOULESTIN Marcel		1936	Oradour (Orbagnac)
BOUILIERE Marie		1872	Oradour
BOUILIERE Odette	Postal worker	1903	Oradour
BOUTAUD Joseph	Shoemaker	1912	Oradour
BOUTAUD Marie	Glovemaker	1908	Oradour
BOUTAUD Marie		1938	Oradour
BRANDY Antoinette	Glovemaker	1923	Oradour
BRANDY Eugenie	Restauranteur	1892	Oradour
BRANDY François	Horticulturist	1899	Oradour (Bellevue)
BRANDY Yvonne	Stationmaster	1918	Oradour
BRASSART Jeanne		1889	Oradour (L'Auze)
BRICAUT Roland		1935	Oradour (Le Glanet)
BRISSARD Catherine		1876	Oradour
BRISSARD Francine	Housekeeper	1924	Oradour
BRISSARD François	Shoemaker	1871	Oradour
BRISSARD Marcel	Wheelwright	1892	Oradour
BRISSARD Marie		1899	Oradour
BROUILLAUD Catherine		1876	Oradour
BROUILLAUD François	Hairdresser	1873	Oradour
BROUILLAUD Jeanne-Marie	Housekeeper	1890	Oradour

BRUGERON André		1938	Oradour (Le Repaire)
BRUGERON René		1934	Oradour (Le Repaire)
BRUN Catherine		1881	Oradour
BUISSON Jeanne		1933	Montreuil-sous-Bois
BUREAU Fernand		1935	Oradour (Le Repaire)
CANIN Guy		1931	Oradour (Le Repaire)
CANITROT Marie-Louise		1890	Montpellier
CARIGNON Jean		1935	Oradour
CHABERT René		1934	Oradour
CHAPEAUD Amélie	Horticulturist	1903	Veyrac
CHAPELLE Jean-Baptiste	Priest	1873	Oradour
CHARTON Simone	Servant	1927	Oradour
CHASTANG Jeanne	Servant	1887	Oradour
CHAUZAT Camille		1937	Oradour (Lespinas)
CHAUZAT Marcelle		1934	Oradour (Lespinas)
CHAZEAUBENEIX Marie	Horticulturist	1910	Javerdat
CHENIEUX Marie		1934	Oradour
CLAVAUD Armand		1862	Oradour
CLAVAUD Lucien		1926	Oradour (La Vallade)
CLAVAUD Marie		1882	Oradour (Le Repaire)
COLDEBOEUF Marie		1897	Oradour
COLIN Bernard		1935	Oradour (La Fauvette)
COLIN Marcelle		1934	Oradour (Le Theil)
COLIN Simone		1936	Oradour (Le Theil)
COLOMBIER Anne-Marie		1874	Oradour
COMPAIN Marie	Confectioner	1904	Oradour
COMPAIN Maurice	Confectioner	1900	Oradour
CORDEAU Bernadette	Dressmaker	1928	Oradour (Les Bordes)
COUDERT Pierre		1938	Oradour (Le Mas-du Puy)
COUTURIER Ginette	Stenographer	1921	Limoges
COUTY Odette	Teacher	1921	Limoges
COUVIDOU Edmond		1937	Oradour (Le Mas-du Puy)
COUVIDOU Georgette		1934	Oradour (Le Mas-du Puy)
COUVIDOU Germaine		1920	Oradour (Le Mas-du Puy)
DAGOURY Léonie	Dressmaker	1915	Oradour
DAGOURY Mélanie	Hotelier	1895	Oradour
DARTHOUT Angèle		1918	Oradour
DARTHOUT Anna		1904	Oradour
DEBUYSER Georges		1937	Oradour (Laplaud)
DEGLANE André	Horticulturist	1870	Oradour (Champ-du-Bois)
DEGLANE Augustin		1887	Oradour
DEGLANE Pierre	Horticulturist	1912	Oradour (Laplaud)
DEGLANE René		1934	Oradour (Les Bordes)
DELAVAULT Yvonne		1931	Oradour
DELHOUME Pierre	Foreman	1890	Limoges
DELHOUME Yvonne	Porcelain worker	1921	Limoges
DELPECH Catherine		1864	Oradour
DEMERY André		1931	Oradour (Bel-Air)
DEMERY Ernest		1933	Oradour (Bel-Air)
DEMERY Henri		1932	Oradour (Le Repaire)
DEMERY Marcelle		1934	Oradour (Le Repaire)
DENIS Léon	Wine Merchant	1884	Oradour
DENIS Lucie		1886	Oradour
DEPIERREFICHE Andrée	Shopworker	1921	Oradour

DEPIERREFICHE Jean	Blacksmith	1884	Oradour
DEPIERREFICHE Marie		1889	Oradour
DESBORDES Lucien		1927	Oradour
DESBORDES Louis	Horticulturist	1932	Oradour
DESBORDES Jean	Horticulturist	1898	Oradour
DESBORDES Jeanne	Horticulturist	1874	Oradour
DESCHAMPS Claudine		1931	Oradour (La Fauvette)
DESCHAMPS Huguette		1936	Oradour (La Fauvette)
DESCHAMPS Maryse		1938	Oradour (La Fauvette)
DESCHAMPS Renée		1879	Oradour
DESCUBES Jacques	Farm Labourer		
DESCUBES Marie		1877	Oradour
DESNOYER André	Shopworker	1929	Oradour
DESNOYER Anne		1906	Oradour
DESNOYER Christian		1934	Oradour
DESNOYER Micheline		1935	Oradour
DESROCHES Marguerite		1874	Oradour
DESOURTEAUX Alice	Grocer	1904	Oradour
DESOUREAUX Anne-Marie		1932	Oradour
DESOUREAUX Etienne	Town clerk	1910	Oradour
DESOUREAUX Geneviève		1935	Oradour
DESOUREAUX Jacques Doctor		1905	Oradour
DESOUREAUX Marie-Anne		1874	Oradour
DESROCHES Georges		1941	Oradour
DESROCHES Ginette		1937	Oradour
DESROCHES Guy		1943	Oradour
DESROCHES Maria	Servant	1919	Oradour
DESSIEX Jacques		1940	Oradour
DESSIEX Marguerite	Horticulturist	1879	Oradour
DESVIGNES Jean		1864	Oradour
DESVIGNES Jean		1931	Oradour
DESVIGNES Madeleine	Butcher	1907	Oradour
DESVIGNES Odile		1937	Oradour
DESVIGNES Yves		1934	Oradour
DOIRE Jean-Baptiste	Well-digger	1875	Oradour
DOIRE Marcelle	Dressmaker	1927	Oradour
DOIRE Marie		1872	Oradour
DOIRE Marguerite		1875	Oradour
DOUTRE Catherine		1891	Oradour
DOUTRE Charles	Carpenter	1926	Oradour
DOUTRE Martial	Carpenter	1893	Oradour
DUCHARLET Marie		1864	Oradour
DUCHARLET Marie	Horticulturist	1879	Oradour
DUCHARLET Marie		1889	Oradour
DUPIC François		1894	Oradour
DUPIC Hubert		1922	Oradour
DUPIC Jean		1897	Oradour
DUPIC Jeanne		1902	Oradour
DUPIC Marie		1902	Oradour
DUPIC Pierre		1922	Oradour
DUQUEROIX Marie-Louise		1902	Oradour
DUQUEROIX Pierre	Labourer	1897	Oradour
DUQUEROY Angélique		1921	Oradour
DUVERNET Adrien	Horticulturist	1924	Oradour (Chez Pinot)

DUVERNET René		1935	Oradour (Chez Pinot)
ENGIEL Raymond		1933	Oradour (La Croix-du-Bois-du-Loup)
ESPINOSA-JUANOS Carmen	Servant	1914	Oradour
FAUCHER Eugénie		1914	Oradour
FAUCHER René		1939	Oradour
FAUGERAS Jean-Claude		1935	Oradour (Le Repaire)
FAURE Aubin		1875	Oradour
FAURE Marie		1871	Oradour
FOREST Dominique		1937	Oradour (Laplaud)
FOREST Michel		1924	Oradour (Laplaud)
FOUGERAS Marie		1882	Oradour
FRANCILLON Gabriel		1856	Oradour
GAILLOT Cécile		1904	Oradour (La Basse-Forêt)
GAILLOT Daniel		1941	Oradour (La Basse-Forêt)
GAILLOT Hubert		1939	Oradour (La Basse-Forêt)
GARAUD André		1936	Oradour (La Fauvette)
GARAUD Martial	Mason	1880	Oradour (Les Bordes)
GARRIGUES Marie		1856	Montpellier
GAUDUFFE Marguerite		1863	Oradour
GAUDY Leonard	Labourer	1874	Oradour
GAUDY Marcelle		1932	Oradour (Laplaud)
GAUDY Maurice		1936	Oradour (Laplaud)
GAUDY Pierre		1934	Oradour (Teineix)
GAUDY Roger		1930	Oradour (Laplaud)
GAUTEYROUX Eugénie		1906	Veyrac
GAZAN Roger	Servant	1927	Oradour
GELAIN Bernard		1928	Oradour
GELAIN Marie-Louise		1923	Oradour
GELAIN Yvonne		1892	Oradour
GEORGES Helene	Horticulturist	1924	Oradour (Orbagnac)
GIACHINO Auguste	Mechanic	1898	Nice
GIBAUD Louise		1889	Limoges
GIL ESPINOZA Francisca		1929	Oradour
GIL ESPINOZA Pilar		1929	Oradour
GIRARD Charles		1902	Oradour
GIRARD Clotilde		1907	Oradour
GIRARD Constant	Horticulturist	1873	Oradour
GIRARD Jannie		1937	Oradour
GIRARD Marie H	Horticulturist	1876	Oradour
GIRARD Yvette		1935	Oradour
GIROUX Pierre		1867	Oradour
GODFRIN Arthur	Baker's hand	1907	Oradour
GODFRIN Claude		1933	Oradour
GODFRIN Georgette		1909	Oradour
GODFRIN Josette		1941	Oradour
GODFRIN Marie		1931	Oradour
GODFRIN Pierre		1933	Oradour
GOUGEON Claude		1940	Oradour
GOUGEON Fernand	Teacher	1911	Oradour
GOUGEON Gérard		1939	Oradour
GOUGEON Marie		1913	Oradour
GOURCEAU Andrée		1934	Oradour
GOUYON Annette		?	Limoges

GRANET Aline		1937	Oradour
GUIONNET Jacqueline		1934	Paris
GUYONNET Marie	Servant	1836	Oradour
HAAS Huguette		1938	Oradour
HAAS Jules-Alphonse		1911	Oradour
HAAS Jules-Paul		1944	Oradour
HAAS Marie-Louise		1916	Oradour
HAAS René		1940	Oradour
HEBRAS Denise		1935	Oradour
HEBRAS Georgette	Nurse	1922	Oradour
HEBRAS Marie		1893	Oradour
HENRY Gilberte		1921	Sartrouville
HENRY Michelle		1942	Sartrouville
HYVERNAUD Albert	Horticulturist	1928	Oradour
HYVERNAUD Andre		1937	Oradour (Le Breuil)
HYVERNAUD André		1940	Oradour
HYVERNAUD Fernand		1898	Panazol
HYVERNAUD Gabriel		1938	Oradour
HYVERNAUD Marcel		1931	Oradour (Le Breuil)
HYVERNAUD Raymonde		1932	Oradour
HYVERNAUD René		1933	Oradour (Mazanty)
HYVERNAUD Roland		1939	Oradour
HYVERNAUD Yvonne		1935	Oradour
ITO Jean	Chimney sweep	1899	Oradour
JOACHIN GIL-EGEA Francoise		1895	Oradour
JOUHAUD Raymond	Packer	1908	Limoges
JOYEUX Catherine		1885	Oradour
JOYEUX Henri		1939	Oradour
JOYEUX Jeanne		1874	Oradour
JOYEUX Marie	Glovemaker	1908	Oradour
JOYEUX Marcel	Mechanic	1921	Panazol
JOYEUX Roger		1940	Oradour
JUGE Anne		1941	Oradour (Les Brégères)
JUGE Gilbert	Horticulturist	1879	Oradour (Les Brégères)
JUGE, Jean		1937	Oradour (Les Brégères)
JUGE Marie		1912	Oradour (Les Brégères)
JUGE Pierre	Horticulturist	1911	Oradour (Les Brégères)
KANZLER Dora		1930	Oradour
KANZLER Joseph	Hairdresser	1893	Oradour
KANZLER Marie		1899	Oradour
KANZLER Simone		1934	Oradour
LABARDE Pierre	Horticulturist	1879	Veyrac
LACROIX Jean		1941	Oradour (Puy-Gaillard)
LACROIX Monique		1943	Oradour (Puy-Gaillard)
LACROIX Olga	Horticulturist	1920	Oradour (Puy-Gaillard)
LACROIX Roland		1944	Oradour (Puy-Gaillard)
LADEGAILLERIE Françoise		1877	Oradour
LAINE Giselle		1541	Oradour
LALUE Léonard	Mason	1873	Oradour
LALUE Marie	Horticulturist	1877	Oradour
LAMARCHE Jean		1874	Oradour
LAMAUD Francois	Horticulturist	1872	Oradour (Bellevue) (xi)
LAMAUD Jean	Horticulturist	1897	Oradour (Bellevue)
LAMAUD Marie	Horticulturist	1897	Oradour (Bellevue)

LAMAUD Marie		1940	Oradour (Bellevue)
LAMIGE Arsene	Baker	1929	Oradour (Chez-Lanie)
LAMIGE Germaine		1938	Oradour (Chez-Lanie)
LAMIGE Marcel		1937	Oradour (Chez-Lanïe)
LANOT Anne		1932	Oradour
LANOT Jeanne		1937	Oradour
LANOT Marguerite	Butcher	1911	Oradour
LATHIERE Marie	Housekeeper	1894	Oradour (Les Brandes)
LAURENT Antonia		1915	Oradour
LAVAUD Jean		1931	Oradour (La Tuilière-des-Bordes)
LAVAUD Louise		1900	Oradour (La Tuilière-des-Bordes)-
LAVERGNE Antoine	Horticulturist	1904	Oradour (Teineix)
LAVERGNE Gilbert		1930	Oradour (Teineix)
LAVERGNE Jean		1879	Oradour (Teineix)
LAVERINE Antoinette		1898	Oradour
LAVERINE Catherine		1862	Oradour
DE LAVERINE Leon		1900	Oradour
DE LAVERINE Mireille		1925	Oradour
DE LAVERINE Thérèse		1926	Oradour
LAVISSE Jean		1931	Oradour
LAURENCE Bernard		1934	Oradour
LAURENCE Genevieve		1937	Oradour
LAURENCE Henri		1889	Oradour
LEBLANC Hortense		1881	Oradour
LEBLANC Jules	Weaver	1875	Oradour
LEBRAUD Emma	Dressmaker	1925	Cieux
LECLERC Anna	Hairdresser	1902	Limoges
LEDOT Maria		1875	Oradour (Le Repaire)
LEDOT Martial	Horticulturist	1881	Oradour (Le Repaire)
LEGER Marcelin	Horticulturist	1879	Oradour
LEGROS Pierre		1923	Reims
LEROY Jeanne		1882	La Chatière
LESPARAT Fernand	Wheelwright	1909	Oradour
LESPARAT Jean	Wheelwright	1881	Oradour
LESPARAT Marcelle	Dressmaker	1912	Oradour
LESPARAT Maria		1888	Oradour
LESPARAT Monique		1931	Oradour
LEVEQUE Marie-Yvonne	Horticulturist	1924	Oradour (Orbagnac)
LEVEQUE Mathilde		1904	Veyrac
LEVIGNAC Charles		1932	Avignon
LEVIGNAC Jean		1928	Avignon
LORENTE Pardo		1935	Oradour
LORICH Angelique		1912	Oradour
LORICH Jacques	Priest	1897	Oradour
LORRAIN Emile		1886	Oradour
LORRAIN Marie		1883	Oradour (Les Brandes)
LORRAIN Paulette		1916	Oradour
MACHEFER Anna		1913	Oradour
MACHEFER Desire		1943	Oradour
MACHEFER Yvette		1933	Oradour
MACHENAUD André	Merchant	1883	Oradour
MACHENAUD Denise		1922	Oradour

MAINGRAUD Marie		1895	Oradour
MAINGRAUD Marius		1890	Oradour
MAIRE Gabriel	Butcher	1908	Oradour
MARTIAL Xavier		1932	Oradour
MASACHS Angélina		1936	Oradour (La Fauvette)
MASACHS Emilia		1933	Oradour (La Fauvette)
MATHIEU Léon	Labourer	1896	Oradour
MATHIEU Marguerite		1899	Oradour
MERCIER François		1861	Oradour (Le Puy-Gaillard)
MERCIER Denis	Horticulturist	1890	Oradour (Le Puy-Gaillard)
MERCIER Jeanne		1867	Oradour
MERCIER Jeanne	Grocer	1894	Oradour
MERCIER Jeanne	Horticulturist	1895	Oradour (Le Puy-Gaillard)
MERCIER Marie	Glovemaker	1907	Oradour (Le Puy-Gaillard)
MERCIER Matthieu		1886	Oradour
MERCIER René	Grocer	1916	Oradour
MERCIER Yvonne		1923	Oradour (Le Puy-Gaillard)
MILORD Juliette		1919	Cullins
MILORD Léon	Innkeeper	1882	Oradour
MILORD Léontine	Ironmonger	1887	Oradour
MILORD Marie		1944	Limoges
MILORD Matthieu		1886	Oradour
MILORD Mélanie	Hotelier	1890	Oradour
MILORD Nicolle		1939	Limoges
MILORD Victor Chef		1914	Oradour
MIOZZO Angèle	Horticuiturist	1929	Oradour (Les Brandes)
MIOZZO Anna		1933	Oradour (Les Brandes)
MIOZZO Armand	Horticulturist	1930	Oradour (Les Brandes)
MIOZZO Bruno	Horticulturist	1929	Oradour (Les Brandes)
MIOZZO Jean		1940	Oradour (Les Brandes)
MIOZZO Louis		1932	Oradour (Les Brandes)
MIOZZO Lucia		1904	Oradour (Les Brandes)
MIRABLON Anna		1885	Limoges
MONDOT Léonard	Labourer	1887	Oradour
MONDOT Léonie		1889	Oradour
MONTAZEAUD Antoine		1892	Oradour
MONTAZEAUD Pierre	Solicitor	1894	Oradour
MOREAU Lucie	Servant		Oradour (Bellevue)
MOREAU Madeleine		1888	Oradour
MOREAU Marguerite		1877	Oradour
MOREAU Pierre	Mason	1877	Oradour
MOREAU Robert		1938	Oradour (Le Mas-du-Puy)
MOREAU Roger		1934	Oradour (Les Bordes)
MORLIERAS Catherine	Hotelier	1898	Oradour
MORLIERAS Irène		1927	Oradour
MOSNIER Marguerite		1887	Oradour
NEUMEYER Emile	Semiriarist	1923	Cellule
NEUMEYER Odile	Servant	1911	Oradour
NICOLAS Jeanne		1934	Oradour
PALLIER Françoise		1909	Paris
PALLI-ER Huguette		1936	Paris
PALLIER Yves		1938	Paris
PASCAUD Denise		1911	Oradour

Name	Occupation	Year	Place
PASCAUD Jean-Louis		1941	Oradour
PASCAUD Marcel	Pharmacist	1912	Oradour
PASQUET Marie	Horticulturist	1896	Javerdat
PECHER Marguerite		1911	Veyrac
PENOT Robert		1931	Oradour (Bellevue)
PERETTE Louis		1896	Oradour
PERETTE Lucie		1890	Oradour
PETIT Marcelle	Hairdresser	1918	Oradour
PETIT Anne		1887	Oradour
PEYROUX Amélie	Horticulturist	1923	Oradour (Chez Gaudy)
PEYROUX Guy		1943	Oradour (Chez Gaudy)
PICAT Germaine		1930	Oradour (Orbagnac)
PICAT Maurice	Businessman	1883	Oradour
PICAT Mélanie		1891	Oradour (Le Mas-du-Puy)
'M PICAT'S SERVANT'		1904	Oradour
PIDANCE Françoise		1882	Oradour
PINEDE Carmen		1904	Oradour
PINEDE Gabrielle		1880	Oradour
PISTER Auguste	Wheelwright	1873	Qradour
PISTER Lucette		1942	Oradour
PISTER Marie		1912	Oradour
PISTER Mélanie		1880	Oradour
PISTER Victorine		1884	Oradour
POUTARAUD Andrée		1933	Oradour
POUTARAUD Danielle		1942	Oradour
POUTARAUD Marcel		1934	Oradour
POUTARAUD Odette		1942	Oradour
POUTARAUD Renée		1912	Oradour
POUTARAUD Suzanne		1935	Oradour
POUTARAUD Yvette		1937	Oradour
PRADIGNAC Anne	Horticulturist	1877	Saint Brice (La Malaise)
RAINIER François	Porcelain Artist	1910	Limoges
RAMBERT Josianne		1939	Oradour
RAMNOUX Albertine	Dressmaker	1901	Oradour
RAMNOUX Claude		1938	Oradour (Les Bordes)
RAMNOUX Jean	Sabot maker	1904	Oradour
RATIER Anne		1938	Oradour (Orbagnac)
RATIER Marie	Horticulturist	1917	Oradour (Orbagnac)
RAYNAUD Bernard		1941	Oradour
RAYNAUD Edith		1935	Oradour (La YTalade)
RAYNAUD Irène		1937	Oradour
RAYNAUD Lucien	Baker	1913	Oradour
RAYNAUD Marguerite		1853	Oradour
RAYNAUD Simone	Baker	1891	Oradour
REDON Irène	Grocer	1925	Oradour
REDON Marie		1873	Oradour
RENAUD Annie		1940	Oradour
RENAUDIN Bernadette		1937	Oradour
RENAUDIN Jules	Blacksmith	1902	Oradour
RESTOUEIX Hubert		1934	Oradour
RIBIERE Marceline		1903	Limoges
RICARD Christian		1931	Oradour (La Valade)
RICHARD André	Solicitor's clerk	1910	Limoges
RICHARD Jean		1937	Oradour (La Valade)

Name	Occupation	Year	Place
RIVES Marie		1876	Oradour
ROBERT Marguerite		1878	St Victurien
ROBY Anna	Horticulturist	1885	Oradour (Le Repaire)
ROBY Marcelle		1938	Oradour (Le Repaire)
ROBY Pierre		1923	Oradour (Le Repaire)
ROUFFANCHE Andrée	Horticulturist	1926	Oradour (Chez Gaudy)
ROUFFANCHE Jean	Horticulturist	1920	Oradour (Chez Gaudy)
ROUFFANCHE Simon	Horticulturist	1891	Oradour (Chez Gaudy)
ROUMY Albert	Student	1921	Oradour
ROUMY Catherine	Horticulturist	1874	Oradour (Les Brandes)
ROUMY Marie		1878	Oradour
ROUSSEAU Jeanne	Teacher	1896	Oradour
ROUSSEAU Léonard	Teacher	1895	Oradour
ROUSSEAU Marguerite	Student	1923	Oradour
ROUSSEAU Pierre		1928	Oradour
ROUSSY Michel		1938	Oradour (Les Cros)
RULIERE Marie		1885	Limoges
SADRY Andrée	Servant	1929	Oradour
SANSONNET Marguerite		1877	Saint-Bric (La Malaise)
SANTANBIEN Henri		1882	Oradour
SANTANBIEN Madeleine		1886	Oradour
SANTROT Jules	Tailor	1878	Oradour
SANTROT Paul	Tailor	1906	Oradour
SAUVIER Marguerite	Dressmaker	1891	Limoges
SAUVIER Paul	Shoemaker	1885	Limoges
SENON Anna		1874	Oradour
SENON Francois	Horticulturist	1866	Oradour
SENON Francoise	Horticulturist	1874	Oradour (Puy-Gaillard)
SENON Jean	Horticulturist	1889	Oradour
SENON Louise		1893	Oradour
SENON Maria	Horticulturist	1893	Oradour
SENON Marie		1864	Oradour
SENON Martial	Cooper	1886	Oradour
SENON Martial	Roadman	1892	Oradour (Le Repaire)
SENON Marguerite	Horticulturïst	1864	Oradour
SERANO-PARDO Armonia		1941	Oradour
SERANO-PARDO Astor		1943	Oradour
SERANO- PARDO Paquita		1943	Oradour
SERANO-ROBLES José	Teacher	1915	Oradour
SERRANO Maria		1913	Oradour
SIMON Marguerite		1932	Oradour (Les Bordes)
SIRIEIX Jean		1867	Oradour
SIRIEIX Jean		1873	Oradour
TELLES Armonia		1926	Oradour
TELLES Dominguez		1890	Bellac
TELLES Maria		1913	Oradour
TELLES Miguel		1933	Oradour
TELLES Philibert		1942	Oradour
TESSAUD Paul	Accountant	1922	Oradour
TEXEREAU Jean		1941	Oradour
TEXEREAU Josette		1936	Oradour
TEXEREAU Henri	Wine Merchant	1908	Oradour
TEXIER Jean		1939	Oradour

TEXIER Jean-Camille		1916	Oradour
TEXIER Louise		1893	Oradour
TEXIER Marie		1914	Oradour St Brice (La Malaise)
TEXIER Marie-Louise		1914	Oradour
TEXIER ?		1940	Oradour
TEXIER ?		1942	Oradour
TEXIER ?			
THIBAULT Lucien		1932	Oradour (Orbagnac)
THOMAS Anna		1892	Oradour
THOMAS Anne		1939	Les Carderies
THOMAS Arthur		1934	Cieux
THOMAS Jean		1874	Oradour
THOMAS Jean		1930	Les Cardieres
THOMAS Madeleine		1939	Les Cardieres
THOMAS Marguerite	Servant	1919	Oradour
THOMAS Marie	Hotelier	1882	Oradour
THOMAS Marie	Horticulturist	1886	Oradour (LeMas-du-Puy)
THOMAS René		1939	Oradour (LeMas-du-Puy)
THOMAS Thérèse	Horticulturist	1918	Oradour (LeMas-du-Puy)
THOMAS ? Madame		1874	Oradour (LeMas-du-Puy)
THOMAS ?		1867	Oradour
THOMASINA Madeline		1936	Oradour (Les Bordes)
TROUILLAUD Renée		1926	Oradour (Les Bordes)
TROUILLAUD Roger		1916	Oradour
VALENTIN Marie		1893	Oradour
VAUCHAMP Michele		1937	Oradour (Les Bordes)
VERGNAUD Anna	Horticulturist	1897	Oradour
VERGNAUD François	Head waiter	1901	Oradour
VERGNAUD Jean	Horticulturist	1896	Oradour
VERGNAUD Marie	Milliner	1905	Oradour
VEVAUD Gilberte		1937	Oradour (LeMas-du-Puy)
VEVAUD Marie	Horticulturist	1907	Oradour (LeMas-du-Puy)
VEVAUD René		1935	Oradour (LeMas-du-Puy)
VIGNAL Sophie		1880	Oradour
VIGNAL Sophie		1880	Oullieres (Rhone)
VIGNAUD Marie- Louise	Servant	1923	Oradour (Les Brégères)
VILLATTE Aimée		1915	Oradour
VILLATTE Amedée	Inspector	1917	Limoges
VILLATTE Christian		1944	Limoges
VILLATTE Christiane		1924	Limoges
VILLATTE Mélanie	Tobacconist	1895	Oradour
VILLATTE Pierre		1862	Oradour
VILLATTE Pierre	Tobacconist	1895	Oradour
VILLEGER Guy	Horticulturist	1927	Oradour (Masset)
VILLEGER Jean	Horticulturist	1902	Oradour (Masset)
VILLEGER ?	Horticulturist	1928	Oradour (Masset)
VINCENT Jean-Paul	Horticulturist	1942	Oradour
VINCENT Raymonde	Teacher	1920	Oradour

INDEX